History of Iran

From the Persian Empire to the Islamic Revolution - A Clear and Captivating Guide to Persia and Modern Iran

Samuel Corwin

Table of Contents

Introduction
The Day Everything Changed
(1979 Revolution)

On February 11, 1979, Iran transformed overnight from a monarchy to an Islamic republic. The streets of Tehran erupted in celebration as the 2,500 year old institution of kingship collapsed. This was not just another regime change; it was a complete revolution that would reshape the Middle East, challenge Western influence, and redefine Iran's relationship with the world.

The Iranian Revolution was the culmination of decades of resentment against foreign interference, authoritarian rule, and rapid modernization, which many Iranians felt threatened their cultural and religious identity. This revolution was led not by generals or political parties, but by religious clerics who mobilized millions through mosques and Islamic networks.

This introduction examines the critical moments of 1979 - the streets filled with protesters, the Shah's desperate flight into exile, and Ayatollah Khomeini's triumphant return. To understand why this revolution matters, we must also recognize its roots in centuries of Persian history, foreign domination, and the enduring power of Shi'i Islam as a force for both resistance and unity.

The events of 1979 continue to influence global politics today, explaining Iran's complex relationship with the West, the rise of political Islam, and the ongoing tensions that define the modern Middle East.

The Streets of Revolution

By late 1978, Iran's cities had become battlegrounds of peaceful resistance. Millions - students, workers, merchants, and religious leaders - took to the streets demanding change. What began as protests against the Shah's policies grew into a movement that paralyzed the country.

The strikes were transformative. Oil workers stopped production, government employees refused to work, and bazaar merchants closed their shops in solidarity. The infrastructure ground to a halt, and the Shah's government became ineffectual.

These were not disorderly mobs. Although clashes with security forces occurred, the protests were organized, disciplined, and united by a demand to end Mohammad Reza Shah Pahlavi's rule. Mosques served as organizing centers, and religious leaders coordinated demonstrations, providing moral authority to the movement.

The Shah's security forces, once feared for their brutality, faced a dilemma: fire on their own people or disobey orders. As defections increased, the regime's power crumbled. The streets belonged to the protesters, and their message was clear - Iran would no longer tolerate authoritarian rule or foreign interference.

By January 1979, the momentum was unstoppable. The revolution moved beyond demands for reform; the people wanted complete transformation, willing to risk everything to achieve it.

The Fall of the Shah

On January 16, 1979, Mohammad Reza Shah Pahlavi left Iran, officially for "medical treatment" and vacation. It was clear he was fleeing into exile, abandoning the Peacock Throne his father had seized in 1925.

The Shah's departure marked the end of an era. For 37 years, he ruled Iran with increasing authoritarianism, backed by Western powers - particularly the United States and Britain. He modernized the country's infrastructure and military, but at a tremendous cost. His secret police, SAVAK, brutally suppressed dissent, and his rapid

Westernization programs alienated traditional and religious Iranians who felt their culture was under threat.

The Shah's relationship with the United States was both a strength and weakness. American support had maintained his power since 1953 when the CIA helped overthrow Iran's democratically elected Prime Minister Mohammad Mossadegh. By 1979, even President Jimmy Carter recognized that the Shah's position was untenable.

As the Shah's plane departed, Iranians celebrated. The symbol of monarchy and foreign domination was gone. Yet uncertainty remained. What would replace the old order? Who would lead the new Iran?

The Pahlavi dynasty, which had promised to restore Persian greatness and modernize Iran, ended not in triumph but with a ruler fleeing his own people. The 2,500 year tradition of Persian kingship collapsed under its contradictions.

The Return of Ayatollah Khomeini

On February 1, 1979, Ayatollah Ruhollah Khomeini returned to Tehran after 14 years in exile. An estimated three to five million Iranians lined the streets from the airport to the city center in one of the largest gatherings in history.

Khomeini was not a typical revolutionary leader. At 76, this senior Shi'i cleric, with his austere lifestyle and uncompromising principles, was the revolution's moral authority. From exile in Iraq and later France, he coordinated opposition to the Shah through sermons smuggled into Iran and distributed via mosque networks.

His message resonated: Iran must be free from foreign domination, governed by Islamic principles, and led by those who understood the people's spiritual and cultural needs. Unlike secular opposition groups, Khomeini offered a complete vision - not just the end of the Shah, but the creation of an Islamic governance system.

The crowds greeting him were diverse. Religious conservatives, leftist students, middle-class professionals, and working-class Iranians all saw in Khomeini a leader who could unite them against the old regime. Various resistance groups - from Islamic organizations to communist factions - endorsed his leadership, at least temporarily.

Ten days after his return, on February 11, 1979, the monarchy officially fell. Khomeini moved swiftly to establish a new government, though the exact nature of the Islamic republic would take months to define. What was clear: Iran had chosen a radically different path, challenging both regional powers and Western influence.

Why This Moment Matters

The Iranian Revolution of 1979 was a pivotal moment in modern history, with consequences that continue to shape our world today.

First, it demonstrated that religious movements could successfully challenge secular, Western-backed governments. This inspired Islamic movements across the Muslim world, changing how political scientists understood revolution. The model wasn't Marxist or nationalist - it was religious.

Second, it fundamentally altered the balance of power in the Middle East. Iran transformed from America's closest regional ally into its most vocal opponent. This shift affected everything from oil markets to regional conflicts, creating tensions that persist decades later.

Third, the revolution influenced American politics directly. The subsequent hostage crisis, where Iranian students seized the U.S. Embassy in Tehran and held 52 Americans for 444 days, dominated the final year of Jimmy Carter's presidency and contributed to Ronald Reagan's election victory in 1980.

Fourth, it established a new form of government: the Islamic republic. Khomeini's concept of velayat-e faqih (guardianship of the Islamic jurist) created a system where religious authorities held ultimate power over elected officials - a unique hybrid challenging both traditional monarchies and secular democracies.

Finally, the revolution represented Iran's assertion of sovereignty and cultural identity after decades of foreign interference. For Iranians, 1979 meant reclaiming their destiny from outside powers who had manipulated their country since the 19th century. This desire for independence and respect continues to drive Iranian foreign policy.

Understanding 1979 is essential for understanding contemporary Iran, Middle Eastern politics, and the complex relationship between religion and revolution in the modern world.

A Story That Begins 2,500 Years Earlier

To understand why the 1979 Revolution happened and why it took the form it did, we must recognize that Iranian history stretches back millennia. The revolution wasn't just about rejecting the Shah - it was about reclaiming a Persian identity that had survived empires, invasions, and foreign domination for over two thousand years.

Ancient Persia was one of history's great civilizations. The Achaemenid Empire (550-330 BCE) ruled from India to Egypt, creating sophisticated administrative systems and promoting religious tolerance. Even after Alexander the Great's conquest, Persian culture endured through the Parthian and Sassanian empires. This deep historical memory gave Iranians a sense of civilizational pride that never disappeared.

The Arab conquest in the 7th century CE brought Islam to Persia, but Iranians maintained their distinct identity by adopting Shi'i Islam - a minority branch that emphasized justice, resistance to oppression, and the rightful leadership of the Prophet Muhammad's family. This religious choice became central to Iranian identity and would prove crucial in 1979.

For centuries, Iran faced interference from foreign powers. In the 19th and early 20th centuries, Britain and Russia competed for control over Iranian territory and resources. The 1953 CIA-backed coup that overthrew Prime Minister Mossadegh and consolidated the Shah's power was just the latest example of outside manipulation.

By 1979, Iranians had endured enough. The revolution drew on this long history - the pride of ancient Persian civilization, the resistance tradition within Shi'i Islam, and the bitter memory of foreign interference. Khomeini and the revolutionaries weren't just creating something new; they were drawing on centuries of Iranian experience and identity.

This historical depth explains why the revolution succeeded and why it took an Islamic form. Iranians weren't simply rejecting monarchy - they were asserting their right to determine their own destiny, free from foreign control, guided by their own cultural and religious traditions.

Common Misconceptions About the 1979 Revolution

Misconception 1: The revolution was purely religious from the start

Reality: The revolution united diverse groups - religious conservatives, leftists, liberals, and nationalists. Many secular Iranians supported Khomeini because he represented opposition to the Shah, not necessarily because they wanted an Islamic government. The religious nature of the final government emerged gradually after the Shah's fall.

Misconception 2: All Iranians supported the Islamic republic

Reality: While millions participated in overthrowing the Shah, significant disagreements emerged about what should replace him. Many secular revolutionaries, women's groups, and ethnic minorities later felt betrayed when the Islamic republic consolidated power and implemented strict religious laws.

Misconception 3: The Shah was simply a dictator with no support

Reality: The Shah had genuine supporters, particularly among the urban middle class, military officers, and those who benefited from modernization programs. However, his repressive tactics, corruption, and perceived subservience to foreign powers alienated enough Iranians to make his position untenable.

Misconception 4: The United States could have prevented the revolution

Reality: By late 1978, the revolution had such broad support that military intervention would have required massive force and likely sparked civil war. The Carter administration faced an impossible situation - supporting the Shah risked American lives and credibility, while abandoning him meant losing a strategic ally.

Misconception 5: The revolution was anti-modern or backward-looking

Reality: Revolutionaries weren't rejecting modernity itself, but rather Western-imposed modernization that ignored Iranian culture and sovereignty. Many revolutionaries were educated, urban Iranians who wanted development on their own terms, not dictated by foreign powers.

Quick Summary: Key Takeaways

- **January-February 1979**: Mass protests and strikes paralyzed Iran, forcing Shah Mohammad Reza Pahlavi into exile on January 16, 1979.

- **February 1, 1979**: Ayatollah Ruhollah Khomeini returned to Tehran after 14 years in exile, greeted by millions of supporters.

- **February 11, 1979**: The monarchy officially collapsed, ending 2,500 years of kingship in Iran and establishing an Islamic republic.

- **Root causes**: Decades of resentment against authoritarian rule, foreign interference (especially by Britain and the U.S.), and rapid Westernization that threatened Iranian cultural and religious identity.

- **Unifying force**: Shi'i Islam provided the organizational structure and moral authority that united diverse opposition groups against the Shah.

- **Global impact**: The revolution transformed Middle Eastern politics, challenged Western influence, and influenced the 1980 U.S. presidential election through the subsequent hostage crisis.

- **Historical context**: The revolution drew on centuries of Persian civilization, Islamic tradition, and bitter memories of foreign domination dating back to the 19th century.

- **Lasting significance**: 1979 established a new model of religious governance and continues to shape Iran's relationship with the world today.

PART 1
THE DNA OF IRAN

Chapter 1
What Makes Iran... Iran?

Iran is one of the world's oldest continuous civilizations, yet it remains widely misunderstood. Unlike many nations with recently formed identities, Iran's sense of self stretches back millennia. Its geography has significantly influenced its politics, and its name reflects complex layers of identity. Remarkably, it has absorbed conquests while maintaining cultural continuity, a feat almost unparalleled in human history.

This chapter delves into the fundamental elements that define Iran: the physical landscape that isolated and protected it, the evolution from "Persia" to "Iran," and the cultural resilience that enabled Persian identity to endure Arab conquest, Mongol devastation, and modern revolution. Understanding these foundations is essential to comprehending Iran's role in both ancient and contemporary history.

We will explore how mountains and deserts created natural barriers influencing Iranian strategy for centuries, the reasons behind the country's name change in 1935, and how Iranian civilization often absorbed invaders rather than being erased by them. By the end of this chapter, you'll understand the geographic, cultural, and historical forces that make Iran distinct from its neighbors and explain its enduring influence in the Middle East.

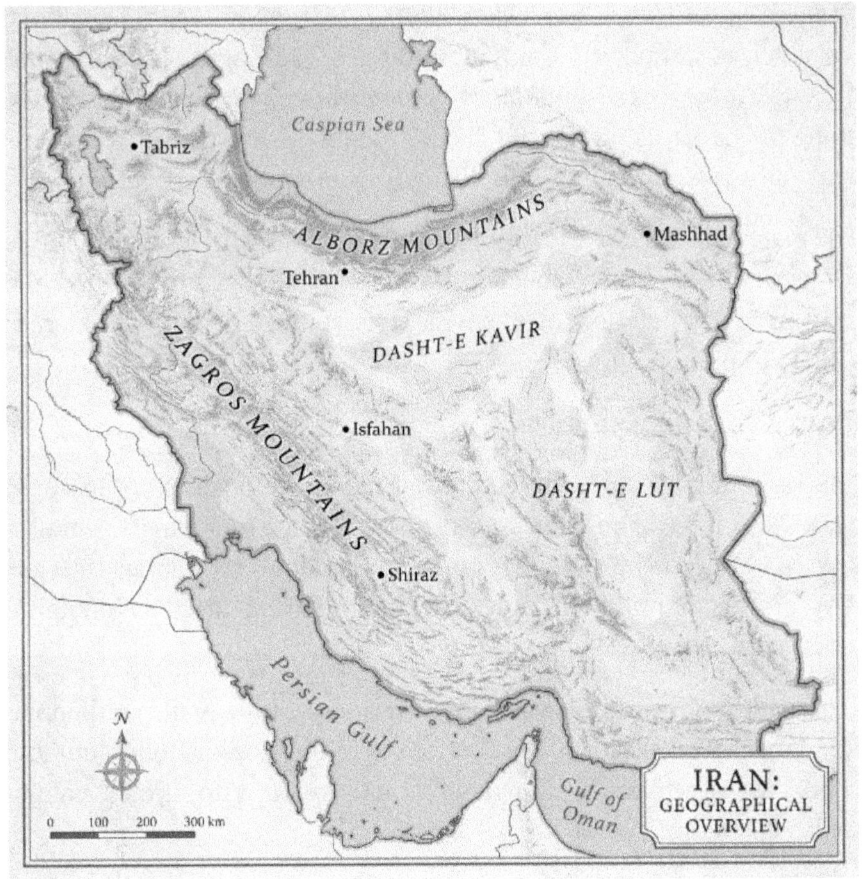

Map of Iran highlighting mountains and deserts

Iran sits at the crossroads of the Middle East, Central Asia, and South Asia, making it strategically valuable yet perpetually vulnerable to invasion. However, Iran's geography has also provided natural defenses, allowing it to maintain independence while other civilizations fell.

The Iranian Plateau

At the heart of Iran is an elevated plateau, averaging 4,000 feet above sea level, surrounded by mountain ranges: the Zagros Mountains to the west, the Alborz Mountains to the north, and the Kopet Dag range along the northeastern border. These mountains have created barriers against invaders, making Iran difficult to conquer completely.

The plateau is largely arid, with only about 10% of Iran's land suitable for agriculture. This concentration of habitable land dictated the location of population centers, making control of water resources critical to political power.

Strategic Chokepoints

Iran's geography has fostered natural defensive positions. Mountain passes limit invasion routes, with the Zagros Mountains forming a barrier between the Mesopotamian plains and the Iranian interior. Any army attempting to invade from the west faced challenging terrain and extended supply lines.

This geography influenced Iranian military strategy for millennia. Iranian rulers learned to use the terrain, fortifications, and strategic depth, often retreating into mountainous regions to stretch enemy supply lines thin.

Access to Trade Routes

Despite its barriers, Iran controlled key trade routes connecting East and West. The Silk Road passed through Iranian territory, bringing wealth and cultural exchange. This strategic location allowed Iranian rulers to benefit from commerce while maintaining defensive advantages.

The combination of natural barriers and strategic location bestowed Iran with a unique geopolitical position: isolated enough to preserve independence but connected enough to influence regional affairs.

Mountains, Deserts, and Isolation

Iran's landscape is dominated by extremes, shaping settlement patterns, economic development, and political fragmentation throughout its history.

The Mountain Barriers

The Alborz Mountains run along Iran's northern edge, reaching heights above 18,000 feet, with Mount Damavand as the highest peak. The Zagros Mountains form an arc along the western and southwestern borders, creating a formidable barrier between Iran and Mesopotamia.

These mountains not only defended against invasion but also isolated Iranian regions. Travel between cities required navigating difficult passes, contributing to Iran's history of regional power centers.

Desert Interior

Central Iran contains two major deserts: the Dasht-e Kavir and the Dasht-e Lut, among the hottest and driest places on Earth. Summer temperatures in the Dasht-e Lut can exceed 160°F at ground level.

These deserts made the Iranian interior largely uninhabitable, prompting population centers to develop along the plateau's edges where water was available. Cities like Tehran, Isfahan, and Shiraz grew in regions with access to mountain runoff or qanats - underground water channels.

Water as Power

In Iran's arid climate, control of water equated to control of population and agriculture. Iranian engineers developed qanat systems to transport water from mountain sources to cities and farmland, requiring centralized organization and maintenance. Rulers who managed water infrastructure effectively gained power.

Isolation and Identity

Iran's geographic isolation helped preserve cultural continuity. While empires rose and fell, the Iranian plateau remained distinct, helping maintain Persian language, customs, and identity even under foreign rule.

Persia vs. Iran: Names and Identity

The country referred to as Iran today was internationally known as Persia until 1935. This name change reflects complex questions of identity, nationalism, and self-perception versus foreign perception.

The Origin of "Persia"

The name "Persia" originates from "Pars" (or "Fars"), a region in southwestern Iran. The ancient Achaemenid Empire began in Pars, and Greek historians referred to the entire empire as "Persia" based on this provincial name.

For over two millennia, Europeans used "Persia" to describe the region and its people. To outsiders, "Persia" evoked images of ancient empires and exotic culture.

What Iranians Called Themselves

Iranians called their country "Iran," meaning "land of the Aryans." This name appears in ancient texts, reflecting an identity beyond a single province. "Aryan" here refers to ancient Indo-European peoples with no connection to later racial theories.

The 1935 Name Change

In 1935, Reza Shah Pahlavi requested that foreign governments use "Iran" instead of "Persia" in official correspondence, reflecting rising nationalism and a desire to emphasize Iran's pre-Islamic heritage.

This change was partly influenced by contemporary European ideas about race and nationalism. Reza Shah sought to associate Iran with modern nations and distance it from "Oriental" stereotypes.

Modern Usage

"Iran" is the official name today, but "Persian" remains correct for language, culture, and historical references. Iranians speak Persian (Farsi), not Iranian. The dual naming reflects Iran's complex identity: ancient yet modern, Eastern yet distinct.

A Civilization That Survives Conquest

Iran's distinct ability to absorb conquerors while maintaining cultural continuity is noteworthy. Conquerors often adopted Persian systems, culture, and even language.

Arab Conquest and Cultural Survival

In the 7th century CE, Arab armies conquered the Sasanian Empire, introducing Islam and Arabic script. Yet, Persian language and culture survived. Within two centuries, Persian re-emerged as a literary language, with poets like Ferdowsi preserving pre-Islamic history in works such as the Shahnameh.

The Iranian bureaucratic class maintained influence by integrating Persian systems into the Arab administration, proving indispensable to their rulers.

Mongol Devastation and Recovery

The Mongol invasions in the 13th century were catastrophic, with cities destroyed and populations massacred. Yet, the Mongols eventually adopted Persian culture, with the Ilkhanate employing Persian administrators and patronizing Persian arts.

The Pattern of Absorption

This pattern repeated throughout history. Turkic tribes, the Safavid Dynasty, and others adopted and enriched Persian culture. Iran's ability to culturally absorb conquerors is due to:

- **Advanced administration**: Persian bureaucratic sophistication was unmatched.

- **Literary tradition**: Persian poetry and literature held prestige.

- **Religious adaptability**: Iranians adapted religious contexts while preserving cultural practices.

- **Geographic continuity**: The Iranian plateau remained a unique, unifying region.

Modern Continuity

This pattern persists. Even the 1979 Islamic Revolution, which rejected monarchy and Western influence, maintained Iranian identity and language.

The Foundations of Iranian Identity

Iranian identity is anchored in interconnected foundations that have remained stable despite political changes.

Language as Cultural Anchor

The Persian language is central to Iranian identity, maintaining continuity from ancient to modern times. Persian literature, including works by Ferdowsi and Rumi, provides cultural cohesion even during political fragmentation.

Pre-Islamic Heritage

Iran's pre-Islamic past is a source of pride. The Achaemenid and Sasanian Empires are celebrated for their power and cultural achievements. Despite the 1979 Revolution's emphasis on Islamic identity, pre-Islamic symbols like Nowruz remain important.

Shia Islam as Unifying Force

Twelver Shia Islam, established as the state religion by the Safavid Dynasty, distinguished Iran from its Sunni neighbors. This identity was politically reinforced by the 1979 Revolution and subsequent events like the Iran-Iraq War.

Adaptation and Resilience

Iranian identity is characterized by adaptability. It has absorbed conquerors while preserving core cultural elements, allowing survival even as others fell.

Legacy and Continuity

The legacies of past dynasties continue to shape modern Iran. Nationalist sentiments, modernization efforts, and political transformations have been influenced by historical experiences, maintaining Iran's unique position in the region.

Common Misconceptions About Iranian Identity

1. **Iran and Persia are the same**: "Persia" was a Western name; "Iran" is the indigenous name.

2. **Iranians are not Arabs**: Iranians speak Persian, an Indo-European language, and have a distinct cultural identity.

3. **Iran's identity isn't purely Islamic**: Iranian culture includes pre-Islamic traditions and retains significant Persian influences.

4. **Geography made Iran difficult to conquer**: Its natural defenses created by mountains and deserts resisted many invaders.

5. **Persian culture survived Arab conquest**: It became a major cultural language and influenced the Islamic world widely.

Quick Summary

Key Takeaways:

- **Geography**: Iran's mountains, deserts, and plateau provided natural defenses and shaped its political strategies.

- **Cultural Preservation**: Isolation of the Iranian plateau preserved Persian identity through conquests.

- **Name Change**: The 1935 switch from "Persia" to "Iran" was a nationalist move.

- **Cultural Absorption**: Iran absorbed conquerors culturally while adopting political and religious systems.

- **Language and Literature**: Persian serves as a cultural anchor.

- **Historical Heritage**: Both pre-Islamic and Shia Islamic traditions contribute to Iranian identity.

- **Survival through Change**: Iranian sovereignty persisted through colonial pressures and revolutionary shifts.

- **Modernity and Tradition**: Iran's consistence in identity amidst modernization and political upheaval sets it apart.

Chapter 2
The First Civilizations

Long before the great Persian empires captured the world's imagination, the Iranian Plateau was home to ancient peoples who laid the foundations for one of history's most influential civilizations. This chapter explores the earliest societies that shaped Iran - from the enigmatic Elamites who built sophisticated cities in the shadow of the Zagros Mountains, to the nomadic Indo-Iranian tribes who would transform the region forever.

Understanding these first civilizations is essential to grasping how Persian culture emerged. The Elamites were not simply conquered and forgotten; their administrative systems, artistic traditions, and language continued to influence Persian rulers long after their decline. Meanwhile, the arrival of Indo-Iranian peoples around 2000 BCE introduced new languages, religious concepts, and social structures that would define Iranian identity for millennia.

This chapter examines four critical developments: the rise and achievements of the Elamite civilization, the migration of Indo-Iranian peoples onto the plateau, the tribal power structures that preceded formal empires, and the gradual emergence of a distinct Persian cultural identity. By 559 BCE, when Cyrus the Great founded the Achaemenid Empire, he wasn't creating something entirely new - he was building upon centuries of cultural evolution, blending Elamite sophistication with Indo-Iranian traditions to forge the world's first superpower.

The World of the Elamites

Around 2700 BCE, while Egypt's pyramids rose and Mesopotamian city-states competed for dominance, a sophisticated civilization flourished in what is now southwestern Iran. The Elamites built their society in Khuzestan and throughout the Zagros Mountains, creating one of the ancient world's most enduring yet least understood cultures.

Geography and Settlement

The Elamites occupied a strategic position between Mesopotamia and the Iranian Plateau. Their heartland in Khuzestan provided fertile land, and their mountain territories offered mineral resources and defensive advantages. This geography allowed them to thrive as both farmers and traders, connecting Mesopotamia with Central Asia.

Unlike their Mesopotamian neighbors, the Elamites left fewer written records, making their history more challenging to reconstruct. What we know comes primarily from Mesopotamian sources and archaeological evidence from sites like Susa, their primary capital.

Political Organization

Elamite civilization wasn't a single, continuous empire but rather a series of kingdoms and confederations over two millennia. Their political structure often featured a unique system where power was shared between multiple rulers or family members.

The Elamites frequently interacted with Mesopotamian powers - sometimes as allies, often as rivals. They successfully resisted domination for centuries, even sacking the Babylonian city of Ur around 2000 BCE and carrying off the famous law code of Hammurabi.

Cultural Achievements

The Elamites developed their own writing system distinct from Mesopotamian cuneiform, though they also adopted cuneiform for diplomatic and administrative purposes. Their art featured distinctive styles, particularly in metalwork and cylinder seals.

Their religious practices centered on unique deities, emphasizing goddess worship. They built impressive ziggurats and temples, showcasing sophisticated architectural knowledge.

The Neo-Elamite Period and Legacy

By 800 BCE, the Elamites entered the Neo-Elamite period as Indo-European speaking Iranian peoples migrated into the region. Elamite civilization gradually transformed and merged with these newcomers.

The Elamite influence on Persian civilization was lasting. When Cyrus the Great established the Achaemenid Empire, he chose Susa - the ancient Elamite capital—as one of his administrative centers. The Achaemenid bureaucracy continued using the Elamite language for record-keeping, demonstrating the civilization's enduring administrative sophistication.

The Arrival of Indo-Iranian Peoples

Around 2000 BCE, a migration began that would reshape the Iranian Plateau and influence the Near East. Indo-Iranian peoples, part of the larger Indo-European language family, moved onto the plateau, bringing languages, religious concepts, and social structures that would define the region for millennia.

The Great Migration

The Indo-European peoples originated from the Eurasian steppes, though their exact homeland is debated. Around 2000 BCE, these groups began diverging into distinct branches. The Western Group moved into Europe, becoming the ancestors of Greeks, Romans, Celts, and Germanic peoples. The Eastern Group, known as Indo-Iranians, moved southward and eastward.

This migration wasn't an invasion but a gradual process spanning centuries. Some Indo-Iranians moved into the Indian subcontinent, developing Vedic culture. Others, the Iranian branch, settled on the Iranian Plateau.

Who Were the Indo-Iranians?

These migrants were primarily pastoral, skilled in horse breeding and chariot warfare. They organized into tribal groups led by warrior aristocracies. Their society valued martial prowess, cattle wealth, and complex rituals.

They brought with them a language that evolved into the Iranian language family, including Old Persian, Avestan (the language of Zoroastrian scriptures), and eventually modern Persian, Kurdish, and others.

Religious and Cultural Contributions

The religious worldview of the Indo-Iranians profoundly influenced Persian culture. They worshipped nature deities and practiced elaborate fire rituals. Concepts of cosmic order, truth (asha), and the struggle between good and evil forces - ideas later crystallized in Zoroastrianism - had roots in Indo-Iranian thought.

Their oral traditions included epic poetry celebrating heroic deeds and legendary kings, contributing to Persian literary culture, notably the Shahnameh (Book of Kings).

Interaction with Existing Populations

The Indo-Iranian arrival didn't displace existing populations like the Elamites. Instead, a complex process of cultural blending occurred. The newcomers adopted local practices while introducing their own traditions. In some regions, they dominated politically; in others, they merged with existing power structures.

By 800 BCE, cultural blending had accelerated as larger numbers of Iranian-speaking peoples settled throughout the plateau.

Foundation for Future Empires

The Indo-Iranian migration created the cultural and linguistic foundation for later Iranian empires. The Median Empire, emerging in northwestern Iran, represented the first major political organization of these Iranian peoples. The Medes would be succeeded by the Achaemenids, who built upon both Indo-Iranian traditions and the administrative sophistication inherited from civilizations like Elam.

Tribal Societies and Early Power Structures

Before empires rose, the Iranian Plateau was dominated by tribal societies with complex power structures. Understanding these organizations is crucial to comprehending how the first Iranian empires emerged.

Tribal Organization

Indo-Iranian society was organized around kinship groups and clans forming larger tribal confederations. These were sophisticated hierarchies with well-defined roles.

Each tribe was led by a chief or king whose authority derived from hereditary right and leadership ability. Below the chief were warrior aristocrats who owned land, controlled herds, and led followers. These nobles formed a military elite dominating tribal politics.

Common people included farmers, herders, and craftsmen. While not equal to the aristocracy, they had recognized rights within tribal law and could own property.

The Role of Warriors

Warfare and martial skill were central to tribal culture. Young aristocrats trained extensively in horsemanship, archery, and combat. Success in battle brought honor, wealth, and influence.

Tribes competed for grazing lands, water resources, and trade routes.

These conflicts weren't chaotic - they followed recognized rules and customs. Alliances formed and dissolved based on strategic interests and kinship ties.

Religious Authority

Alongside political and military leaders, priests held significant power. They performed rituals, maintained oral traditions, and interpreted divine will. Religious specialists weren't separate from political life - they legitimized rulers and sanctified important decisions.

Fire rituals were particularly important, with priests maintaining sacred fires symbolizing cosmic order and divine presence.

From Tribes to Kingdoms

Over time, some tribal confederations grew more powerful. Successful chiefs expanded authority over multiple tribes, creating proto-kingdoms. This process accelerated as settled agriculture became important and as contact with established civilizations introduced new administrative concepts.

The Median Empire, which emerged in northwestern Iran, represented the culmination of this process. The Medes successfully united multiple Iranian tribes under a single authority, creating the first significant Iranian political entity.

Tribal Legacy in Imperial Structures

Even after empires emerged, tribal structures didn't disappear. The Achaemenid Empire, founded by Cyrus the Great in 559 BCE, retained elements of tribal organization. Persian nobles traced their authority through ancient clan connections. The empire's military relied heavily on tribal contingents led by hereditary chiefs.

This blending of tribal traditions with imperial administration created a distinctive Persian political culture - one that balanced centralized authority with respect for traditional power structures.

The Birth of Persian Culture

Early Persian artifacts

Persian culture didn't emerge suddenly with the founding of the Achaemenid Empire in 559 BCE. Instead, it developed gradually through centuries of cultural blending, as Indo-Iranian traditions merged with Elamite sophistication and neighboring influences.

Cultural Synthesis

The foundation of Persian culture rested on the fusion of multiple traditions. From Indo-Iranians came language, religious concepts, epic traditions, and social structures. From the Elamites came administrative expertise, architectural techniques, and artistic traditions. Mesopotamian influences included writing systems and legal concepts.

This was a selective adoption and transformation of elements, creating something genuinely new.

Language and Identity

The Persian language, part of the Iranian branch of Indo-European languages, became a crucial marker of identity. Old Persian developed as the language of the elite, though the region's multilingual nature meant that Elamite, Akkadian, and others continued in use for specific purposes.

Language carried values, stories, and worldviews. Persian epic traditions, passed down orally, celebrated heroic kings and the importance of truth and justice.

Religious Foundations

Persian religious thought evolved from Indo-Iranian roots. While Zoroaster's life timing is debated, the religious concepts that would become Zoroastrianism - including truth (asha), the cosmic struggle between good and evil, and individual moral choice - were forming during this period.

Fire remained central to religious practice, symbolizing purity and divine presence. Rituals emphasized maintaining cosmic order and supporting the forces of good against chaos and falsehood.

Social Values

Persian culture emphasized virtues that would characterize the civilization for centuries:

- Truth-telling and keeping one's word
- Martial courage and skill
- Loyalty to kin and king
- Hospitality and proper conduct
- Justice and fair dealing
- Respect for hierarchy while protecting the weak

These values weren't merely ideals - they shaped legal systems, political expectations, and daily behavior.

Artistic Expression

Persian artistic traditions drew on multiple sources while developing distinctive styles. Metalwork, textile production, and architectural decoration showed Elamite influences and new Iranian elements. The emphasis on symmetry and stylized motifs characterized Achaemenid art.

The Role of Kingship

Persian concepts of kingship blended tribal leadership traditions with established models. The ideal king was both a warrior and a just ruler, maintaining cosmic order and protecting his people.

When Cyrus the Great founded the Achaemenid Empire, he built on these evolving concepts, presenting himself as the fulfillment of Persian cultural ideals - a just king and a successful warrior.

A Culture Ready for Empire

By the mid-sixth century BCE, Persian culture had matured to support imperial ambitions. The Persians possessed:

- A sophisticated language and literary tradition
- Evolved religious and ethical concepts
- Administrative knowledge from Elam
- Military traditions from their Indo-Iranian heritage
- A concept of kingship for large-scale rule

The stage was set for the Achaemenid Empire to emerge as the world's first superpower.

Common Misconceptions About Early Iranian Civilizations

Misconception 1: The Persians simply conquered and replaced earlier peoples

Reality: Persian culture emerged through centuries of cultural blending. The Elamites weren't eliminated; their systems and language continued during the Achaemenid period. The process was synthesis, not simple replacement.

Misconception 2: Pre-imperial Iran was primitive and tribal

Reality: While tribal structures existed, the Iranian Plateau was home to sophisticated civilizations like Elam for over two millennia before the Achaemenid Empire. These societies had complex political systems, writing, monumental architecture, and extensive trade networks.

Misconception 3: Indo-Iranian migration was a sudden invasion

Reality: The arrival of Indo-Iranian peoples was a gradual process spanning centuries, beginning around 2000 BCE. It involved migration, settlement, and cultural exchange, not a single military conquest.

Misconception 4: Persian culture began with Cyrus the Great

Reality: Cyrus built upon centuries of cultural development. Persian language, religious concepts, social structures, and values had been evolving long before the Achaemenid Empire was founded in 559 BCE.

Misconception 5: The Elamites left no lasting influence

Reality: Elamite civilization profoundly influenced later Persian empires. The Achaemenids used Susa as an administrative capital, employed Elamite for bureaucratic records, and adopted Elamite administrative techniques. The cultural continuity was significant.

Quick Summary

Key Takeaways:

- The Elamite civilization (from 2700 BCE) was a sophisticated society in southwestern Iran that influenced later Persian empires through administrative systems, artistic traditions, and continued use of the Elamite language.

- Around 2000 BCE, Indo-Iranian peoples began migrating onto the Iranian Plateau, bringing new languages, religious concepts, and social structures that would define Iranian identity.

- Early Iranian society was organized around tribal structures with warrior aristocracies, religious specialists, and complex systems of alliances and confederations.

- The Median Empire represented the first major political unification of Iranian tribes, setting the stage for the later Achaemenid Empire.

- Persian culture emerged through the synthesis of Indo-Iranian traditions, Elamite sophistication, and influences from Mesopotamian civilizations.

- By 559 BCE, when Cyrus the Great founded the Achaemenid Empire, he was building upon centuries of cultural evolution rather than creating something entirely new.

- The blending of tribal traditions with administrative sophistication created a distinctive Persian political culture that balanced centralized authority with respect for traditional power structures.

- Persian values emphasizing truth, justice, martial courage, and proper kingship were well-established before the rise of the first Persian empire.

PART 2
THE AGE OF EMPIRES

Chapter 3
Cyrus the Great — The First Superpower

In the mid-sixth century B.C.E., a transformative force emerged from the Iranian plateau. Cyrus the Great molded a collection of Persian tribes into history's first true superpower - an empire stretching from the Mediterranean to Central Asia. Unlike conquerors who ruled by fear, Cyrus pioneered an approach built on tolerance, respect, and diplomacy.

His methods established an empire that dominated the Near East for over two centuries and set governance standards that influenced civilizations for millennia. This chapter explores how Cyrus built an unprecedented empire, managed its vast diversity, and why his legacy endures.

The Rise of Cyrus

Cyrus II, known as Cyrus the Great, hailed from the Achaemenid dynasty in what is now southern Iran. His lineage connected him to the powerful Persians and the Medes, through his mother, Mandane, daughter of Astyages, the last Median king.

While details of Cyrus's early life are sparse, by the mid-sixth century B.C.E., he emerged as the leader of the Persians, who were then subordinate to the Medes.

The Decisive Moment

Around 549 B.C.E., Cyrus defied Persian subordination by rebelling against Astyages. Many Median nobles, dissatisfied with Astyages, defected to Cyrus, enabling a strategic unification rather than mere conquest.

By defeating Astyages, Cyrus merged the Medes and Persians, forming the Achaemenid Empire. This new entity possessed significant military might and dominated the Iranian plateau.

Building Momentum

Cyrus, leading a united Median and Persian force, established himself as a legitimate successor to existing powers. This strategy defined his reign as he expanded beyond the Iranian plateau toward Anatolia and Mesopotamia.

Conquests and Expansion

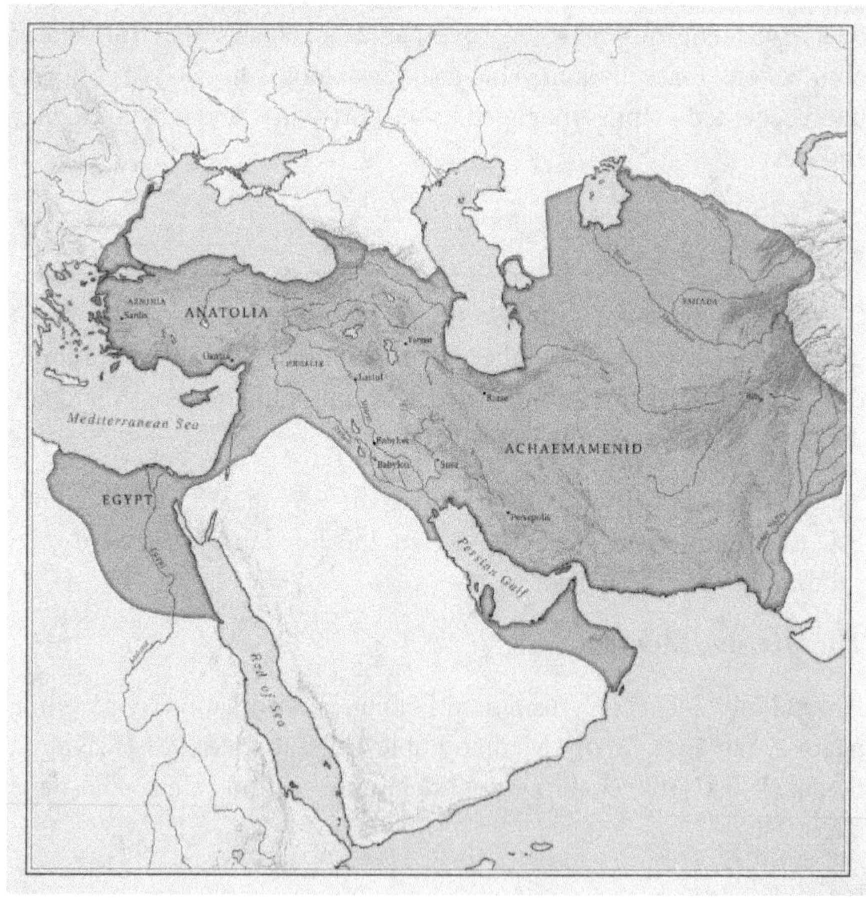

Map of the Achaemenid Empire

Between 549 and 530 B.C.E., Cyrus transformed his base into a vast empire through strategic conquests, combining military brilliance with diplomatic acumen.

The Conquest of Lydia

Cyrus's first major external conquest targeted Lydia in western Anatolia. Known for its wealth, Lydia controlled crucial trade routes. Cyrus captured Sardis, the Lydian capital, extending Persian control and initiating contact with Greek city-states.

The Babylonian Campaign

In 539 B.C.E., Cyrus conquered Babylon, the heart of Mesopotamia. Rather than besiege its fortified walls, Persian forces diverted the Euphrates River, entering through the riverbed with minimal destruction.

Cyrus entered Babylon as a liberator, aligning himself with Marduk, Babylon's chief god, ensuring a smooth transition of power.

Expanding the Borders

Cyrus extended Persian influence eastward into Central Asia, creating an empire stretching from the Aegean to the borders of India. This vast entity required innovative governance strategies.

Military Innovation

Cyrus developed a professional, multi-ethnic army, integrating strengths from various warrior traditions, setting a template for future imperial armies.

Governing an Empire

Conquering an empire was one challenge; governing it posed another. Cyrus faced the task of managing vast territories with diverse peoples and traditions.

The Policy of Tolerance

Cyrus's key innovation was his policy of tolerance. Unlike earlier conquerors, he allowed conquered populations to retain their customs and religions, strategically minimizing rebellion and securing cooperation.

Administrative Autonomy

Cyrus employed a decentralized administration, granting autonomy to regional rulers while they acknowledged Persian supremacy and paid tribute. This system relied on a network of roads and communication to maintain balance between central control and regional flexibility.

Religious Policy

Cyrus's religious tolerance was notable. He restored temples and religious statues, earning loyalty from religious communities. The Cyrus Cylinder records his policy of allowing displaced peoples to return home, contrasting sharply with earlier empires' deportation policies.

Building Imperial Infrastructure

Cyrus initiated infrastructure development essential for empire management, including road networks and communication systems, foundations expanded by his successors.

Cyrus Cylinder artifact

Cyrus the Great died around 530 B.C.E., likely in battle on the empire's eastern frontier. His reign, though brief, had a lasting impact.

Immediate Impact

Cyrus left a functional empire that his successors expanded. His son Cambyses II conquered Egypt, and later rulers refined the administrative systems Cyrus pioneered.

Model of Governance

Cyrus established governance models combining military strength, administrative flexibility, and cultural tolerance, influencing subsequent empires, including Rome.

Cultural Memory

Cyrus's reputation transcended cultures. Greek historians depicted him as a model ruler, Jewish tradition honored his support for their return to Jerusalem, and Persian culture celebrated him as an empire's founder.

Historical Significance

Cyrus demonstrated that empires could thrive through respect and diplomacy, showing cultural diversity as an imperial strength. His governance approach continues to inform political thinking on managing diverse populations.

The empire he founded was the first true superpower, shaping ancient world structures and providing models for future civilizations.

Common Misconceptions About Cyrus the Great

Misconception 1: Cyrus conquered purely through military force

Cyrus's success also relied on diplomacy and strategic alliances, with many territories joining voluntarily.

Misconception 2: Cyrus's tolerance was purely idealistic

His tolerance was pragmatic, reducing resistance and easing governance.

Misconception 3: The Persian Empire was ethnically Persian

The empire was multi-ethnic from its inception, with contributions from various peoples.

Misconception 4: Cyrus invented tolerance

While not the concept's inventor, Cyrus applied tolerance as a deliberate imperial strategy.

Misconception 5: All of Cyrus's conquests were peaceful

Cyrus's approach to treatment after victory was innovative, not conflict avoidance.

Quick Summary

Key Takeaways:

- Cyrus united the Medes and Persians, founding the Achaemenid Empire as a new superpower.

- His major conquests included Lydia and Babylon, expanding Persian control significantly.

- He pioneered cultural and religious tolerance, allowing conquered peoples to maintain their traditions.

- His administration granted regional autonomy, balancing local flexibility with central authority.

- The Persian Empire became the largest political entity of its time, encompassing diverse cultures.

- Cyrus's legacy influenced future empires and governance models balancing strength and diplomacy.

- Remembered positively across cultures, reflecting the impact of his policies.

- The empire lasted until Alexander the Great's conquest, demonstrating the durability of Cyrus's foundations.

Chapter 4
How Persia Ruled the World

The Persian Empire didn't just conquer territories - it mastered the art of governing them. Under Darius the Great, Persia transformed from a collection of conquered lands into history's first true superpower, stretching from Egypt to India. This achievement was remarkable not just for its military might, but also for an innovative system of administration that balanced central authority with local autonomy.

Between 522 and 486 BCE, Darius revolutionized imperial governance. He created structures that influenced empires for centuries: standardized currency, efficient communication networks, legal frameworks that respected local traditions, and a policy of religious tolerance. These mechanisms enabled diverse peoples to coexist under one banner without constant rebellion.

This chapter explores how Persia ruled its vast empire. We'll examine the administrative machinery that kept the empire running, the infrastructure that connected distant provinces, the religious policies that maintained peace, and daily life for those living under Persian rule. Understanding these systems reveals why the Persian Empire lasted over two centuries and shaped governance long after its fall.

The Administrative System

Darius the Great inherited an empire difficult to control. Previous rulers had conquered vast territories, but governing them effectively was challenging. Around 500 BCE, Darius implemented reforms that transformed Persian administration into the ancient world's most sophisticated system.

The Satrapy System

Darius expanded the empire's administrative divisions from approximately 20 satrapies to 36. Each satrapy functioned as a province governed by a satrap - a regional governor with significant authority. This wasn't simple delegation; it was strategic decentralization.

Satraps collected taxes, maintained order, commanded local military forces, and administered justice according to local customs. This autonomy allowed the empire to govern regions with diverse cultures, languages, and legal traditions without imposing a single rigid system.

However, Darius included checks to prevent satraps from becoming too independent. Royal inspectors, known as "the King's Eyes and Ears," traveled throughout the empire monitoring satrap activities, creating an accountability mechanism that balanced local autonomy with central oversight.

Standardization and Communication

A significant innovation was establishing Imperial Aramaic as the administrative language across the empire. While local populations continued speaking their native languages, government officials used Aramaic for official correspondence. This created consistency while respecting linguistic diversity.

Darius also harmonized the empire's diverse legal traditions into a coherent imperial framework. Rather than replacing local laws entirely, he incorporated elements from various legal cultures within the empire. Local courts continued operating within this broader system.

Economic Innovation

Darius introduced the first standardized currency system across the empire - the gold daric and silver siglos. Before this, different regions used various forms of payment, complicating trade and tax collection. Standardized currency revolutionized economic activity, making transactions simpler and more reliable.

This administrative system succeeded because it was pragmatic rather than ideological. Darius recognized that effective governance required flexibility, not uniformity.

Roads, Communication, and Trade

An empire spanning three continents needed more than good administration - it required infrastructure to connect its distant parts. Darius understood that communication and trade networks were essential for maintaining control and promoting prosperity.

The Royal Road

The crown jewel of Persian infrastructure was the Royal Road, stretching approximately 1,600 miles from Sardis to Susa, one of the empire's capitals. It was an engineered highway with regular stations and organized support systems.

The road served multiple functions. Militarily, it allowed rapid troop movement. Administratively, it enabled swift communication between the capital and provinces. Economically, it facilitated trade across and beyond the empire.

The Postal System

Along the Royal Road, Darius established relay stations approximately every 15 miles. Royal messengers could change horses at these stations, allowing messages to travel the road in about seven days - a journey that took ordinary travelers three months.

This postal system was exclusively for government use, carrying royal decrees and intelligence reports. The speed and reliability of communication provided gave Persian rulers unprecedented control over their vast territory.

Trade Networks

The infrastructure Darius created had profound economic effects. Merchants used the Royal Road and other highways to move goods between East and West. The standardized currency eliminated exchange complications, while the empire's stability made long-distance trade safer.

These communication and trade networks integrated the empire's diverse regions, creating connections that made rebellion less attractive. Provinces benefited from access to markets and goods, giving them economic incentives to remain within the empire.

Religion and Tolerance

Nothing distinguished Persian rule more than its approach to religion. In an era when conquerors often imposed their gods, Persia took a radically different path of tolerance and respect.

The Policy of Religious Freedom

Persian rulers, particularly Darius, actively promoted religious tolerance. Local populations could worship their gods, maintain temples, and practice customs without interference.

This tolerance had practical foundations. The Persian Empire encompassed numerous distinct peoples. Imposing a single religion would have sparked rebellions. Tolerance maintained peace and legitimacy.

Supporting Local Religions

Persian kings went beyond mere tolerance - they actively supported local religious institutions. They funded temple construction, participated in ceremonies, and presented themselves as legitimate rulers within local frameworks.

In Babylon, Persian kings assumed traditional titles. In Egypt, they were depicted as pharaohs. Such adaptability allowed them to be seen as legitimate rulers rather than occupiers.

Cyrus the Great's decree allowing Jews to return to Jerusalem and rebuild their temple wasn't unique; it reflected standard Persian policy of supporting local religious institutions.

Zoroastrianism and Imperial Identity

While promoting tolerance, Persian rulers followed Zoroastrianism, a monotheistic religion emphasizing truth and justice. Zoroastrian principles influenced governance, particularly justice and lawful rule.

However, Persians didn't impose Zoroastrianism, maintaining a distinct imperial identity without requiring religious uniformity.

The Prohibition of Slavery

Persians prohibited slavery, a remarkable stance in the ancient world. This policy reflected Zoroastrian ethical principles and distinguished Persian rule, contributing to the empire's stability.

Life Inside the Empire

Daily life under Persian rule varied by location, social status, and occupation. Yet certain features of governance shaped experiences across the empire.

Local Autonomy and Continuity

For most, Persian conquest didn't dramatically alter daily life. Local governments continued functioning, and traditional laws remained in effect. Farmers, craftsmen, and merchants conducted business as before.

This continuity was deliberate policy. As long as provinces paid taxes and maintained order, Persian authorities interfered little with local affairs.

Economic Opportunities

The empire's infrastructure and stability created economic opportunities. Merchants could travel safely across vast distances.

Standardized currency simplified transactions. Highways reduced travel time and costs.

Artisans and craftsmen benefited from increased trade, and agricultural producers gained access to larger markets. The empire's prosperity supported specialized craftspeople.

Tax Obligations

The primary burden of Persian rule was taxation. Each satrapy owed tribute to the imperial treasury, calculated on the region's wealth. Satraps collected these taxes through various means.

Tax rates varied and were generally considered reasonable. The system was predictable, though collection could be harsh if satraps sought personal enrichment.

Military Service and Security

The empire maintained security with professional troops and local forces. Some regions provided military contingents.

For most, Persian rule meant greater security, deterring invasions and suppressing banditry. Trade routes were safer, and regional conflicts decreased, creating stability.

Cultural Exchange

Living within a vast empire exposed people to diverse cultures, ideas, and practices. Travelers, merchants, and officials carried goods, stories, and innovations. Cities became cosmopolitan.

This exchange enriched life, blending artistic styles and ideas. While local identities remained strong, awareness of the broader world grew.

Common Misconceptions About Persian Rule

Misconception 1: The Persian Empire was a brutal, oppressive tyranny.

Reality: Persian rule was tolerant and pragmatic, allowing local autonomy and religious freedom.

Misconception 2: Satraps were essentially independent kings.

Reality: Satraps had authority but were balanced by royal inspectors and central oversight.

Misconception 3: The Persian Empire imposed its religion on conquered peoples.

Reality: Persia promoted religious tolerance and supported local religious traditions.

Misconception 4: The Royal Road was only for military use.

Reality: It facilitated civilian trade and travel, connecting East and West.

Misconception 5: Life under Persian rule was uniform across the empire.

Reality: The empire's diversity defined it. Local customs and traditions varied widely.

Quick Summary

Key Takeaways:

- Darius expanded the empire to 36 satrapies, creating decentralized governance with central oversight.

- Imperial Aramaic served as the administrative language while preserving local languages and customs.

- The Royal Road and postal system enabled rapid communication across the empire.

- Standardized currency revolutionized trade and economic activity.

- Persian religious tolerance allowed diverse peoples to maintain their traditions.

- Slavery was prohibited, reflecting Zoroastrian ethical principles.

- Local autonomy meant continuity in daily life despite imperial rule.

- Infrastructure and stability created economic opportunities for merchants, artisans, and farmers.

Chapter 5
The Clash with Greece

The Persian Empire's expansion westward brought it into inevitable conflict with the Greek city-states, igniting one of history's most pivotal confrontations. The Greco-Persian Wars (499-449 BCE) were more than mere territorial disputes - they were a collision between two markedly different civilizations. On one side was the vast, centralized Persian Empire under Kings Darius I and Xerxes I; on the other, the fiercely independent Greek city-states, united by culture yet divided politically.

These wars tested Persian imperial ambition and highlighted Greek military innovation and unity. Legendary battles such as Marathon, Thermopylae, Salamis, and Plataea echo through history, marking a Greek victory that preserved their independence and allowed Athens to flourish, ushering in a golden age of democracy, philosophy, and art.

This chapter explores why these powers clashed, how major battles unfolded, what the wars revealed about the limits of empire, and how this conflict created the first clear divide between East and West, shaping centuries of history.

The Causes of Conflict

The roots of the Greco-Persian Wars lay in the Achaemenid Empire's relentless expansion. By the late 6th century BCE, Persian territory stretched from Egypt to India, with the Greek cities of Ionia (modern-day western Turkey) under Persian control. These cities, long tied to mainland Greece, increasingly resented Persian rule.

The Ionian Revolt

In 499 BCE, the Ionian cities rebelled against Persian authority, sparking the Ionian Revolt, which lasted until 493 BCE. The rebels sought support from mainland Greece, with Athens sending ships and soldiers in aid.

Although the revolt was crushed, Athens' involvement infuriated King Darius I. From the Persian perspective, Athens had interfered in imperial affairs and supported rebellion. This intervention transformed a regional uprising into an international crisis.

Persian Motivations

Darius I regarded the Greek city-states as threats to imperial stability. Supporting the Ionian rebels would inspire other subjects to revolt. Additionally, the fragmented Greek world seemed ripe for conquest, promising control over the Aegean region and its trading cities.

Greek Divisions

The Greek city-states were not unified. Athens and Sparta clashed politically, while many smaller cities remained neutral or sided with Persia, seeking gains over their rivals. Initially, this disunity made Greece appear vulnerable.

The Major Battles

The Battle of Marathon (490 BCE)

Darius I's first major invasion in 492 BCE faced logistical challenges, but in 490 BCE, a Persian force of 25,000 landed at Marathon, expecting to march on Athens easily. Instead, 10,000 Athenian hoplites, led by Miltiades, employed tactics that enveloped the Persian army.

The Greeks achieved a stunning victory, inflicting heavy casualties while losing few themselves. This success shocked Persia and showed that Greek hoplites could defeat Persian forces. Tradition holds that a messenger ran from Marathon to Athens to announce the victory, inspiring the modern marathon race.

The Battle of Thermopylae (480 BCE)

After Darius's death, Xerxes I assembled a massive invasion force. In 480 BCE, his army, possibly numbering 100,000 to 300,000, entered Greece.

The Greeks, led by Spartan King Leonidas, made a stand at the narrow pass of Thermopylae with about 7,000 men, including his 300 Spartans. For three days, they held their ground, inflicting severe losses. A traitor revealed a path to outflank them, leading Leonidas to dismiss many but remain with the 300 Spartans and 700 Thespians, who fought to the last.

Though a tactical defeat, Thermopylae symbolized courage and delayed the Persians, proving they could be resisted.

The Battle of Salamis (480 BCE)

After Thermopylae, Persian forces captured Athens. However, Athenian leader Themistocles evacuated the city, banking on naval strength.

Themistocles lured the Persian fleet into the narrow straits of Salamis, where Greek triremes, smaller and more agile, dominated. The Persians suffered catastrophic losses, forcing Xerxes to retreat to Persia.

The Battle of Plataea (479 BCE)

In 479 BCE at Plataea, a Persian army of 50,000, led by Mardonius, faced a united Greek force. The Greeks launched a decisive assault, killing Mardonius and decimating the Persians. Simultaneously, a Greek naval victory at Mycale ended Persian attempts to conquer Greece.

The Limits of Empire

The Greco-Persian Wars highlighted the Achaemenid Empire's limitations against resolute resistance. Despite numerical superiority, Persia faced critical challenges.

Logistical Challenges

Maintaining supply lines across the Aegean and Greece proved taxing. Greek forces, with local knowledge, had shorter supply routes. Losing naval dominance at Salamis forced Xerxes to withdraw.

Military Adaptability

Greek hoplites, organized in phalanx formations, excelled in close combat against Persian troops. Persian doctrine, suited for sprawling plains, couldn't counter Greek tactics.

Greek naval prowess, particularly Athens' fleet, surpassed Persian commanders, who lacked the unity and training of Greek crews.

Political Unity vs. Imperial Diversity

Despite Greek political fragmentation, rivals cooperated against a common threat. Persia, relying on diverse subject peoples, faced internal loyalty issues.

The Persian Empire's vastness couldn't guarantee victory against a determined, tactically superior foe.

The First East–West Divide

The Greco-Persian Wars crystallized a cultural and political divide between East and West.

Democracy vs. Monarchy

Greek writers framed the wars as freedom versus tyranny: the democratic institutions of Athens against a Persian monarchy. This narrative influenced Western political thought deeply.

Cultural Identity

The wars strengthened Greek cultural unity, emphasized against Persian "otherness." The concept of "Hellas" gained clearer definition in opposition to Persia.

Historical Legacy

Historians like Herodotus depicted the wars as crucial to Greek identity, crafting narratives of courage versus excess. This foundational story influenced how civilizations later understood cultural and political conflicts.

Common Misconceptions About the Greco-Persian Wars

Misconception 1: The Persians were barbaric and uncivilized

The Persian Empire boasted advanced administration, architecture, and culture, though Greek propaganda painted it otherwise.

Misconception 2: Greece was unified against Persia

Many Greek city-states were neutral or allied with Persia. Athens and Sparta's unity was temporary.

Misconception 3: The 300 Spartans fought alone at Thermopylae

Around 7,000 Greeks defended Thermopylae initially, with 1,000, including 700 Thespians, fighting alongside the Spartans.

Misconception 4: Persian defeat ended their power

Persia remained a major power for 150 years after the wars. Defeats limited expansion but didn't weaken control over Asia and Egypt.

Misconception 5: The wars were purely about freedom vs. tyranny

The conflicts stemmed from complex causes, including economic and territorial ambitions, beyond mere ideals.

Quick Summary

Key Takeaways:

- The Greco-Persian Wars began with the Ionian Revolt and Athenian support against Persia.

- Major battles included Marathon (490 BCE), Thermopylae (480 BCE), Salamis (480 BCE), and Plataea (479 BCE).

- Greek victory was due to superior tactics, home territory advantages, and cooperation against an existential threat.

- The wars demonstrated Persian expansion limits, revealing that size and resources couldn't guarantee success.

- Persian defeat preserved Greek independence, enabling Athens' Golden Age.

- The wars established a major East-West cultural divide and narratives about freedom versus tyranny, influencing Western identity.

- Persia remained a powerful empire in Asia and the Middle East post-defeat.

- The legacy of these wars shaped later understanding of cultural and political conflicts.

Chapter 6
Collapse and Comeback

The story of ancient Persia is not one of steady decline but of dramatic falls and remarkable resurrections. Few civilizations have experienced such catastrophic defeats only to rise again with renewed strength and identity. This chapter explores three distinct phases in Persian history: the devastating conquest by Alexander the Great that ended the Achaemenid Empire, the emergence of the Parthian dynasty that reclaimed Persian independence, and the powerful Sasanian Empire that would become Rome's greatest rival.

Together, these periods demonstrate an extraordinary pattern of resilience - a civilization that refused to disappear even when conquest seemed absolute.

This cycle of collapse and revival reveals something fundamental about Persian identity. Unlike empires built purely on military might, Persian civilization carried cultural and administrative traditions so deeply rooted that they survived even when political structures crumbled. The Persians would lose their empire, but they would not lose themselves.

The Conquests of Alexander

In 334 BC, a young Macedonian king crossed into Asia Minor with an army of approximately 40,000 men. Alexander III - later called "the Great" - would accomplish what no Greek leader had managed before: the complete destruction of the Persian Empire.

The Fall of an Empire

Alexander's campaign against Persia unfolded with shocking speed. At the Battle of Granicus in 334 BC, he defeated Persian forces in Asia Minor. The following year, at Issus, he routed a much larger Persian army led by King Darius III himself. By 331 BC, Alexander had won the decisive Battle of Gaugamela, effectively ending organized Persian resistance.

The conquest was systematic and devastating. Alexander captured the great Persian capitals one by one: Babylon opened its gates without resistance, Susa surrendered peacefully, but Persepolis - the ceremonial heart of the empire—suffered a different fate. In 330 BC, Alexander's troops looted the city and burned the magnificent palace complex, whether deliberately or accidentally remains debated by historians.

Darius III fled eastward, hoping to regroup his forces. He never got the chance. In 330 BC, his own nobles assassinated him, hoping to win favor with the conqueror. Alexander had achieved what seemed impossible: in less than four years, he had conquered an empire that had stood for over two centuries.

The Hellenistic Transformation

Alexander's conquest was not merely military - it was cultural. He actively promoted the fusion of Greek and Persian cultures, a policy modern historians call Hellenization. He adopted Persian royal customs, wore Persian dress, and married Roxana, a Bactrian princess. He encouraged his officers to marry Persian noblewomen and recruited Persian soldiers into his army.

Greek became the language of administration across the former Persian territories. Greek cities were founded throughout the conquered lands, bringing Greek architecture, philosophy, and religious practices. The gymnasium, the theater, and Greek-style temples appeared in cities from Egypt to Central Asia.

This cultural exchange flowed in both directions. Greeks encountered Persian administrative systems, astronomical knowledge, and artistic traditions. Trade routes that had connected the Persian Empire now facilitated even greater exchange between East and West. Goods, ideas, and people moved more freely than ever before.

The Empire Divided

Alexander died unexpectedly in Babylon in 323 BC, at just 32 years old. He left no clear heir, and his empire immediately fractured. His generals, known as the Diadochi ("Successors"), fought for decades over the spoils.

The former Persian territories were divided among several Hellenistic kingdoms. The Seleucid Empire claimed most of the Iranian plateau and Mesopotamia. Egypt fell to the Ptolemaic dynasty. Smaller kingdoms emerged in Bactria and other regions.

For the Persian people, Alexander's conquest marked a profound disruption. The Achaemenid dynasty was gone. Greek became the language of power. Foreign rulers governed from Greek-style cities. Yet beneath this Hellenistic veneer, Persian culture, language, and identity survived - waiting for the right moment to reassert itself.

The Rise of the Parthians

The Parthian Empire emerged not from the Persian heartland, but from the northeastern frontiers - a reminder that Persian civilization extended far beyond Persis itself.

Origins of the Parthians

The Parthians were originally a nomadic Iranian people from the region of Parthia, southeast of the Caspian Sea. Under Seleucid rule, they remained a distinct group with their own language (a Middle Iranian dialect) and customs. Around 247 BC, a chieftain named Arsaces led a successful revolt against Seleucid authority, establishing what would become the Arsacid dynasty.

The timing was crucial. The Seleucid Empire was weakening, distracted by conflicts in the west and internal power struggles. The Parthians exploited this weakness, gradually expanding their control over the Iranian plateau.

Building an Empire

The Parthian rise was gradual but relentless. Under Mithridates I (ruled 171–132 BC), the Parthians transformed from a regional power into an empire. They conquered Mesopotamia, capturing the ancient cities of Babylon and Seleucia. By 141 BC, they controlled territories stretching from the Euphrates River to the borders of India.

The Parthians developed a distinctive political system. Rather than imposing centralized control like the Achaemenids, they ruled through a federation of semi-autonomous kingdoms and city-states. Local rulers maintained significant authority as long as they acknowledged Parthian supremacy and paid tribute.

Masters of Cavalry Warfare

The Parthians revolutionized military tactics with their cavalry-based army. They became famous for two types of mounted warriors: heavily armored cataphracts who charged enemy lines, and light horse archers who employed hit-and-run tactics.

The "Parthian shot" - firing arrows backward while retreating on horseback - became legendary. This technique allowed Parthian forces to defeat larger armies through mobility and harassment rather than direct confrontation. In 53 BC, at the Battle of Carrhae, Parthian cavalry annihilated a Roman army led by Crassus, killing or capturing nearly 40,000 Roman soldiers.

Rome's Eastern Rival

The Parthian Empire became Rome's primary rival in the East, a position it would hold for nearly five centuries. Unlike Rome's other enemies, the Parthians could not be conquered. Multiple Roman invasions failed, and the Euphrates River became an accepted boundary between the two superpowers.

This rivalry was not purely military. The Parthians controlled the Silk Road trade routes connecting Rome with China and India. Silk, spices, and luxury goods flowed through Parthian territory, generating enormous wealth. Both empires understood that war disrupted this profitable trade, leading to periods of uneasy peace punctuated by border conflicts.

Cultural Revival

Under Parthian rule, Persian culture experienced a renaissance. While the Parthians adopted some Hellenistic elements, they actively promoted Iranian traditions. The Persian language regained prominence. Zoroastrianism flourished again as the dominant religion. Persian artistic styles reemerged, blending with Hellenistic influences to create distinctive Parthian art.

The Parthians saw themselves as heirs to the Achaemenid legacy, even though they came from a different Iranian ethnic group. They minted coins featuring Arsaces I, their founder, and adopted the title "King of Kings," echoing Achaemenid royal terminology.

The Power of the Sasanian Empire

In AD 224, a new Persian dynasty emerged that would surpass even the Parthians in power and cultural achievement: the Sasanian Empire.

A New Dynasty

Ardashir I, a Persian noble from the province of Persis (the original Persian heartland), rebelled against Parthian rule. In AD 224, he defeated the last Parthian king, Artabanus IV, and established the Sasanian dynasty, named after his grandfather Sasan.

The Sasanians explicitly claimed descent from the Achaemenids and positioned themselves as restorers of true Persian greatness. Unlike the Parthians, who had come from the periphery, the Sasanians emerged from the same region that had produced Cyrus the Great - a fact they used to legitimize their rule.

Imperial Reorganization

The Sasanians created a highly centralized state that rivaled Rome in administrative sophistication. They divided the empire into provinces governed by appointed officials directly responsible to the king. They established a professional bureaucracy, standardized taxation, and maintained a standing army.

Under rulers like Shapur I (ruled AD 240–270) and Khosrow I (ruled AD 531–579), the Sasanian Empire reached its peak. Shapur I famously defeated and captured the Roman emperor Valerian in AD 260 - an unprecedented humiliation for Rome. Khosrow I reformed the tax system, patronized learning, and earned the title "the Just."

Cultural Flowering

The Sasanian period witnessed a remarkable cultural renaissance. Zoroastrianism became the official state religion, with a formalized priesthood and religious hierarchy. The Avesta, Zoroastrian sacred texts, were compiled and written down. Magnificent fire temples were constructed throughout the empire.

Sasanian art and architecture achieved new heights. The palace at Ctesiphon featured the largest single-span vault in the ancient world. Sasanian metalwork, textiles, and rock reliefs influenced artistic traditions from Europe to China. The Sasanian royal court became legendary for its splendor, inspiring tales in both East and West.

Rome's Equal

The Sasanian Empire was the only power Rome recognized as an equal. For over four centuries, these two superpowers faced each other across the Mesopotamian frontier. They fought numerous wars, but neither could decisively defeat the other. Their rivalry shaped the ancient world's geopolitics, economics, and culture.

The Sasanians controlled key trade routes and actively promoted commerce. Their silver coins circulated from Britain to China, testimony to their economic reach. Sasanian Persia became a bridge between civilizations, facilitating the exchange of goods, technologies, and ideas across Eurasia.

A Civilization That Refuses to Fall

The pattern is unmistakable: Persian civilization possessed a remarkable capacity for renewal. Alexander's conquest, which should have ended Persian culture, instead led to its eventual resurgence under the Parthians. When the Parthians weakened, the Sasanians emerged to create an even more powerful Persian state.

This resilience stemmed from deep cultural roots - language, religion, administrative traditions, and a strong sense of identity that transcended individual dynasties. Persian civilization was not dependent on any single ruling family or political structure. It was embedded in the land, the people, and their shared heritage.

Even when foreign powers conquered Persian territories, they often adopted Persian administrative methods, employed Persian officials, and absorbed Persian cultural elements. The conquerors, in a sense, became conquered by the civilization they had defeated.

Common Misconceptions

"Alexander destroyed Persian civilization"

Alexander conquered the Persian Empire politically and militarily, but Persian culture, language, and identity survived and eventually reasserted themselves. Within a century of his death, Iranian dynasties ruled much of the former empire again.

"The Parthians were barbarian invaders"

The Parthians were an Iranian people with cultural and linguistic connections to the Persians. They saw themselves as liberators restoring Iranian rule, not foreign conquerors.

"The Sasanians were a completely new civilization"

The Sasanians explicitly positioned themselves as heirs to the Achaemenids, reviving and building upon earlier Persian traditions rather than creating something entirely new.

"Rome always defeated the Persians"

The historical record shows a more balanced picture. The Parthians and Sasanians won numerous victories against Rome, including the complete destruction of Roman armies and the capture of a Roman emperor.

"Persian power ended with the Sasanians"

While the Sasanian Empire fell to Arab conquest in the 7th century AD, Persian cultural influence continued to shape Islamic civilization, and Persian dynasties would emerge again in later centuries.

- **Alexander's conquest (334–330 BC)** destroyed the Achaemenid Empire in less than four years, bringing Greek culture and administration to Persian territories.

- **The Parthian Empire (247 BC–AD 224)** emerged from northeastern Iran, gradually reclaiming Persian independence and becoming Rome's primary eastern rival.

- **Parthian cavalry tactics**, especially the famous "Parthian shot," made them formidable opponents who defeated multiple Roman invasions.

- **The Sasanian Empire (AD 224–651)** restored centralized Persian rule, claimed Achaemenid heritage, and created a sophisticated state that rivaled Rome.

- **Sasanian cultural achievements** included religious formalization, architectural marvels, and artistic innovations that influenced civilizations from Europe to China.

- **Persian resilience** demonstrated that civilization is more than politics - cultural identity, language, and traditions can survive even catastrophic military defeat.

- **The Roman-Persian rivalry** shaped ancient geopolitics for over 700 years, with neither superpower able to decisively defeat the other.

PART 3
THE GREAT TRANSFORMATION

Chapter 7
The Islamic Conquest

The seventh century witnessed a profound transformation in Persian history. In under two decades, the powerful Sasanian Empire – which had endured for over four centuries – succumbed to the expanding Arab Muslim armies. This conquest was not merely a military defeat; it initiated a deep cultural, religious, and political upheaval that would redefine Persia.

The Islamic conquest of Persia, from 633 to 654 CE, was swift yet monumental. The Sasanian Empire, already weakened by enduring wars with Byzantium and internal discord, could not resist the determined Rashidun Caliphate. By 651 CE, the last Sasanian king had fallen, marking the beginning of Persia's integration into the Islamic world.

This chapter explores the fall of a once-mighty superpower, the rapid success of Arab armies, and the embedding of Islam into Persian soil, culminating in a unique blend of Arab and Persian traditions that would influence the Islamic world for centuries.

The Fall of the Sasanian Empire

The Sasanian Empire began the seventh century as a dominant power, rivaling Byzantium. By mid-century, it had vanished. Understanding this rapid collapse requires examining both the empire's vulnerabilities and the relentless pressure exerted by Muslim forces.

A Weakened Giant

Facing the Muslim invasions, the Sasanian Empire was severely weakened. Prolonged wars with Byzantium had depleted its resources and manpower. The final Byzantine-Sasanian war (602-628 CE) was particularly devastating, leaving the empire vulnerable.

Internal instability exacerbated these issues. Political fragmentation and succession disputes weakened the central authority. The Muslim armies encountered an empire struggling to maintain cohesion and effective resistance.

The Last King: Yazdegerd III

Yazdegerd III ascended the throne as the Sasanian Empire faced its greatest challenge. His reign (632-651 CE) was marked by retreat and desperate attempts to rally resistance against the Muslims.

In a bid to counter the threat, Yazdegerd III allied with the Byzantine Empire – Persia's traditional foe—though this unusual alliance ultimately failed to stop the Arab advances.

The Conquest Unfolds

The Muslim conquest began in 633 CE and advanced rapidly. Arab armies, driven by religious zeal and the lure of conquest, systematically expanded into Sasanian territories. Under Caliph Umar, these campaigns were strategically coordinated.

In 638 or 639 CE, Muslim forces launched a major offensive on Fars, a key Persian province, marking the start of sustained pressure on the heartland. Despite their rich military traditions, the Sasanians were continually outmaneuvered.

The death of Caliph Umar in 644 CE did not halt the conquest. By then, the tide had decisively turned in favor of the Muslims.

The Final Battle

The Battle of the Oxus in 651 CE sealed the fate of the Sasanian Empire. Muslim commander Ahnaf ibn Qais led a decisive victory over the remaining Sasanian forces, forcing Yazdegerd III into flight.

Yazdegerd III's death ended the Sasanian dynasty. Attempts by his descendants to restore the empire failed. The Sasanian state, a ruling power since 224 CE, was no more.

Why the Empire Fell

Several factors explain the swift collapse:

- **Exhaustion from wars**: Prolonged conflict with Byzantium drained resources.

- **Internal divisions**: Political instability weakened resistance.

- **Military disadvantages**: Arab forces were more mobile and adaptable.

- **Loss of key territories**: Early defeats deprived the empire of resources and strategic depth.

- **Collapse of central authority**: As the king retreated, provincial resistance fragmented.

The fall of the Sasanian Empire left a power vacuum quickly filled by the Islamic Caliphate, setting the stage for Persia's transformation.

The Expansion of Arab Armies

Map of early Islamic expansion into Persia

The rapid Arab military expansion into Persia remains a remarkable achievement. Within two decades, armies from the Arabian Peninsula conquered territories long resistant to external domination. Understanding this success requires examining their military advantages, strategic approach, and favorable circumstances.

The Rashidun Caliphate's Military Machine

The Rashidun Caliphate emerged as an effective military power following Muhammad's death. Arab armies combined religious motivation with tactical flexibility, creating a formidable force.

The Arabs prioritized mobility, relying on cavalry and rapid movement. This allowed them to outmaneuver the heavier Sasanian forces and exploit weaknesses, quickly concentrating forces to win decisive battles.

Religious conviction provided powerful motivation, as soldiers believed they fought for a divine cause, strengthening their resolve over the war-weary Sasanians.

Strategic Coordination Under Umar

Caliph Umar, ruling during the early conquests (634-644 CE), provided strategic leadership that capitalized on Arab strengths. He coordinated multiple campaigns, ensuring constant pressure on various fronts.

Umar emphasized consolidation as well as conquest, establishing garrison towns to secure territories and extend Arab-Islamic authority.

This systematic approach prevented the Sasanians from regrouping. Each victory eased subsequent advances by securing supply lines and establishing bases for further campaigns.

Key Military Advantages

Arab armies possessed several critical advantages:

- **Mobility**: Light cavalry maneuvered faster than Sasanian heavy forces.

- **Adaptability**: Commanders adjusted tactics to local conditions.

- **Unity of command**: Centralized leadership enabled coordinated strategies.

- **Motivation**: Religious conviction sustained morale.

- **Local support**: Some Persians, disillusioned with Sasanian rule, offered limited resistance.

The Conquest Timeline

The Muslim conquest progressed systematically:

633-638 CE: Initial invasions targeted border regions, weakening defenses. Early victories demonstrated capability and attracted fighters.

638/639 CE: The attack on Fars province brought conflict into Persia's heartland, testing Muslim ability to hold core territories.

640s CE: Sustained campaigns captured cities and defeated Sasanian field armies. Umar's death in 644 did not disrupt momentum.

651 CE: The Battle of the Oxus decisively ended Sasanian resistance, marking the empire's inability to field effective armies.

Garrison Towns and Consolidation

In conquered territories, Arab armies established garrison towns (amsar) that became Islamic authority centers. These towns served multiple purposes:

- Military bases for regional control

- Administrative centers for tax collection and governance

- Cultural hubs fostering Arab-Persian interaction

- Staging areas for further expansion

Garrison towns were vital for maintaining control over vast areas with relatively small Arab populations, projecting power while beginning the cultural integration process.

The Speed of Success

By 654 CE, just two decades after the invasions began, the Muslim conquest of Persia was essentially complete. This rapidity was due to Sasanian weakness, Arab military effectiveness, and strategic coordination.

The conquest's pace left Persian populations little time to organize resistance. With the Sasanian state collapsed, no alternative power structure managed to coordinate opposition, allowing Muslim forces to establish authority quickly across Persian territories.

The Introduction of Islam

Military conquest was only the beginning. Islam's introduction initiated a profound religious and cultural transformation that reshaped Persian identity. This process evolved over centuries, transitioning Persia from a Zoroastrian society to an Islamic one.

The Religious Landscape Before Islam

Before the conquest, Zoroastrianism was the state religion. This ancient faith, with its dualistic worldview, influenced Persian culture for a millennium. The clergy wielded significant political and social power.

Other religious communities, including Christians and Jews, coexisted within the empire. While Zoroastrianism was privileged, Persia was no stranger to religious diversity.

Initial Contact and Conversion

Islam's introduction began during the conquest (633-654 CE) and continued into the early eighth century. Unlike the rapid military conquest, conversion was gradual.

Initially, Arab Muslim conquerors formed a distinct ruling class without forcing conversion. "People of the Book," including Zoroastrians, could maintain their religions by paying a tax (jizya).

This tolerance allowed many Persians to continue their faith initially, with conversions occurring gradually through:

- **Economic incentives**: Muslims paid lower taxes.

- **Social advancement**: Conversion offered opportunities in administration and military.

- **Cultural influence**: Garrison towns exposed Persians to Islamic culture.

- **Intermarriage**: Facilitated cultural and religious exchange.

- **Missionary activity**: Muslims spread teachings.

The Garrison Towns as Cultural Centers

Garrison towns were central to introducing Islam. These settlements fostered sustained Arab-Persian contact, where cultural and religious exchange thrived.

In these towns, Persians encountered Islamic practices, learned Arabic, and absorbed new concepts. Over time, they evolved into cosmopolitan cities blending Arab and Persian cultures.

The Decline of Zoroastrianism

As Islam spread, Zoroastrianism gradually declined due to:

- **Loss of state support**: Without Sasanian patronage, institutions weakened.

- **Economic pressure**: Tax advantages encouraged conversion.

- **Social marginalization**: Increased restrictions on non-Muslims.

- **Cultural shift**: Islam associated with modernity and power.

Conversion varied by region, with some retaining Zoroastrian communities. By the tenth century, Islam dominated most of Persia.

A Unique Persian Islam

Significantly, Persian Islam developed a distinctive character. Persians did not merely adopt Arab culture; they adapted Islam, resulting in:

- Persian Islamic art and architecture

- Contributions to Islamic philosophy and science

- Literary traditions in Islamic contexts

- Unique religious practices blending elements

The introduction of Islam to Persia was an exchange. Persia became Islamic, and Islam became Persian in important ways.

Long-Term Impact

The religious transformation fundamentally altered Persian identity. By the early eighth century, the Islamic era was firmly established, affecting:

- **Personal identity**: Persians increasingly saw themselves as Muslims.

- **Cultural production**: Art and literature reflected Islamic themes.

- **Social structures**: Islamic law shaped daily life.

- **Political legitimacy**: Rulers derived authority from Islam.

Islam's introduction represents a significant religious transformation, creating an Islamic-Persian synthesis that influenced the broader Islamic world for centuries.

A New Political Order

The Islamic conquest established a new political order, transforming governance, power structures, and authority legitimacy. This system blended Arab Islamic principles with Persian administrative traditions, forming a unique governance model.

The End of the Old Order

Yazdegerd III's death and failed restoration attempts marked the definitive end of the Sasanian political system. The Persian monarchy, steeped in divine sanction, ceased to exist.

This collapse created both crisis and opportunity. The Muslim conquerors swiftly established new governance structures to maintain stability.

The Caliphate's Administrative Approach

The Rashidun Caliphate pragmatically absorbed existing Sasanian systems rather than replacing them. Many Persian bureaucrats continued their roles under Muslim rule.

This approach proved effective. Retaining Persian administrators maintained governance continuity, easing the transition for ordinary Persians.

Absorption of Sasanian Systems

Muslim rulers recognized and integrated Sasanian administrative sophistication, including:

- **Tax collection**: Persian methods for revenue assessment.
- **Provincial administration**: Governance structures for distant territories.
- **Record-keeping**: Bureaucratic documentation traditions.
- **Land management**: Agricultural organization and property rights.

This absorption facilitated continuity, softening the drastic changes suggested by conquest.

Military Integration

Maintaining control required local military integration. Persian soldiers who accepted Muslim rule joined the Caliphate's ranks, bringing valuable expertise in warfare and geography.

The Garrison Town System

Garrison towns shaped the new political geography, serving as nodes of Islamic authority. From these centers, governors exerted control over surrounding areas.

Here, the new political order took shape. Islamic law was enforced, taxes collected, and the Caliphate's presence made tangible.

Cultural and Political Synthesis

Over time, the political order evolved, blending Arab Islamic and Persian traditions in:

Language: Arabic dominated administration while Persian reemerged in literature.

Governance philosophy: Islamic concepts of rule merged with Persian kingship ideas.

Court culture: Islamic dynasties adopted Persian ceremonies while maintaining legitimacy.

Artistic expression: Authority expressed in architectural and artistic forms combining elements.

From Conquest to Integration

By the early eighth century, Persia was integrated into the Islamic world. The new order preserved Persian distinctiveness within this integration, fostering a Persian-Islamic identity influencing broader Islamic civilization.

Long-Term Political Impact

The new order's enduring consequences included:

- **End of Persian imperial independence**: Persia was not independently ruled for centuries.

- **Integration into Islamic civilization**: Persian territories were part of a larger world.

- **Administrative influence**: Persian practices spread throughout Islamic lands.

- **Cultural synthesis**: Blending of traditions enriched both cultures.

The Islamic conquest established an order that was neither purely Arab nor traditionally Persian but an Islamic-Persian synthesis defining the region for a millennium.

Common Misconceptions About the Islamic Conquest

Misconception 1: The conquest was completed in a single campaign

The conquest spanned over two decades (633-654 CE) and involved numerous campaigns, not a single decisive effort.

Misconception 2: Persians were forced to convert immediately

Islamic conversion was gradual, occurring over centuries, driven by factors beyond coercion.

Misconception 3: The conquest destroyed Persian culture

Rather than destroying Persian culture, the conquest led to a synthesis where traditions influenced Islamic civilization.

Misconception 4: Arab conquerors completely replaced Persian administrators

Muslims retained many Persian bureaucrats, recognizing the value of established systems.

Misconception 5: The Sasanian Empire fell solely due to Muslim military superiority

The empire's fall was due to multiple factors, including exhaustion from Byzantine wars and internal instability.

Quick Summary

Key Takeaways:

- The Muslim conquest of Persia (633-654 CE) ended the Sasanian Empire, transforming the region politically, religiously, and culturally.

- Yazdegerd III, the last Sasanian king, was defeated at the Battle of the Oxus in 651 CE.

- Arab success was due to mobility, religious motivation, strategic coordination, and Sasanian weakness from Byzantine wars.

- Islam's introduction was gradual, with conversion incentivized over centuries through economic and social factors.

- The new political order absorbed Sasanian systems, creating an Islamic-Persian synthesis.

- Garrison towns facilitated cultural exchange, establishing a distinct Persian-Islamic identity.

- By the early eighth century, Persia was integrated into the Islamic world with unique characteristics.

- The conquest's impact includes the decline of Zoroastrianism, the rise of Islam, and a lasting cultural synthesis affecting Islamic civilization for centuries.

Chapter 8
Losing Power, Keeping Identity

The fall of the Sasanian Empire in 651 CE did not mark the end of Persian civilization. Instead, it began a complex transformation where Persians lost political sovereignty but retained and eventually reasserted their cultural identity within the new Islamic order. This chapter examines how Persians navigated life under Arab rule, first under the Umayyad Caliphate and then under the Abbasids, who rose to power in 750 CE.

Rather than vanishing into the Islamic world, Persian culture, administrative expertise, and intellectual traditions became foundational to the empire that had conquered them. This chapter explores the paradox of political defeat and cultural persistence, demonstrating how Persians adapted to foreign rule while maintaining their distinct identity and ultimately reshaping the empire that governed them.

Life Under the Umayyads

The Umayyad Caliphate, the second major Islamic caliphate after the Prophet Muhammad's death, ruled former Sasanian territories from 661 to 750 CE. For Persians, this period marked a shift from imperial rulers to subjects of an Arab tribal aristocracy.

Political Marginalization

Under Umayyad rule, political power concentrated in Arab hands, particularly among tribal elites from the Arabian Peninsula. The caliphate operated as an Arab empire, with Arabic as the administrative language and Arabs in the highest positions of power.

Persian nobles, who had once commanded armies and governed provinces, found themselves excluded from the upper echelons of power. The Umayyads maintained a hierarchy privileging Arab

Muslims over non-Arab converts (mawali), regardless of their previous status or capabilities.

Economic and Social Structures

The Umayyads implemented a tax system differentiating between Arab Muslims and non-Muslims. Persians who converted to Islam often found that conversion did not bring the economic or social equality they expected. Although the jizya (poll tax on non-Muslims) was replaced by other obligations, mawali still faced discrimination.

Persian landowners generally retained their properties, and the dihqans (local Persian nobility) continued managing agricultural production and tax collection at the local level. This arrangement allowed the Umayyads to govern efficiently without dismantling existing structures.

Cultural Tensions

The Umayyad period saw significant cultural friction. Arab administrators often viewed Persian customs and traditions with suspicion, while Persians resented their subordinate status. The Zoroastrian religion, once the state faith of the Sasanian Empire, faced increasing pressure as Islam became dominant.

Despite these tensions, Persian administrative expertise remained valuable. The Umayyads needed experienced bureaucrats to manage their vast territories, and many Persians found employment in lower administrative positions, preserving governance and record-keeping knowledge.

Seeds of Discontent

Persian dissatisfaction with Umayyad rule grew during this period. The promise of Islamic equality – that all Muslims were equal before God – contrasted sharply with the reality of Arab supremacy. This discontent eventually contributed to the Umayyad downfall, as Persians and other non-Arabs sought a more inclusive political order.

The Abbasid Revolution

In 750 CE, the Abbasid family, descendants of the Prophet Muhammad's uncle, overthrew the Umayyad Caliphate in the Abbasid Revolution. This political transformation fundamentally changed the relationship between Persians and the Islamic state.

The Overthrow

The Abbasid movement gained strength by appealing to widespread discontent with Umayyad rule. They promised a return to Islamic principles of equality and justice, attracting support from mawali, including many Persians marginalized under Arab aristocracy.

The revolution succeeded in 750 CE, establishing the Abbasid Caliphate as the third Islamic caliphate after the Prophet Muhammad. The Abbasids systematically eliminated Umayyad leadership, although one branch escaped to establish a separate caliphate in Spain.

A New Political Order

The Abbasids marked a shift from Arab tribal aristocracy to a more inclusive governance structure. Unlike the Umayyads, the Abbasids actively integrated non-Arabs into political and cultural spheres, recognizing talent and loyalty over ethnic origin.

This change particularly benefited Persians, who possessed sophisticated administrative traditions and educational systems. Persian bureaucrats, scholars, and advisors began ascending to positions of real authority within the caliphate.

Baghdad: A New Center

The Abbasids established their capital in Baghdad in 762 CE, symbolizing the eastward shift of Islamic power. Unlike Damascus, the Umayyad capital in the Arab heartland, Baghdad sat near the former Sasanian capital of Ctesiphon, in the cultural sphere of Persian influence.

Baghdad quickly became the center of what historians call the Islamic Golden Age – a period of extraordinary intellectual and cultural achievement lasting several centuries. Scholars, scientists, poets, and philosophers from across the Islamic world and beyond were drawn to the city.

Persian Participation

Under the Abbasids, Persians found opportunities previously denied to them. They served as viziers (chief ministers), military commanders, provincial governors, and court officials. The Barmakid family, of Persian origin, became particularly influential as viziers to early Abbasid caliphs.

This integration allowed Persians to exercise political power without holding the caliphate itself, which remained an Arab institution. The Abbasid period demonstrated that political sovereignty and cultural influence could exist separately.

Persian Influence in an Arab Empire

The Abbasid Caliphate, though Arab in leadership and Islamic in identity, became increasingly Persian in its administrative practices, court culture, and intellectual orientation.

Administrative Systems

The Abbasids adopted Sasanian administrative models wholesale. The complex bureaucracy that had managed the Persian Empire was ideal for governing the vast Abbasid territories. Persian-style record-keeping, tax collection systems, and provincial administration became standard.

The position of vizier, modeled on the Sasanian office of chief minister, became central to Abbasid governance. Persian bureaucrats brought centuries of administrative expertise, creating efficient systems that allowed the caliphate to function effectively.

Court Culture and Etiquette

Abbasid court life increasingly reflected Persian rather than Arab traditions. The ceremonial practices, hierarchical protocols, and elaborate etiquette of the Sasanian court influenced how caliphs presented themselves and interacted with subjects.

This "Persianization" of court culture elevated the caliphate's prestige and created distance between rulers and subjects, replacing the more accessible Arab tribal leadership style with imperial grandeur.

Language and Literature

While Arabic remained the language of religion and administration, Persian language and literature experienced a renaissance under Abbasid rule. Persian scholars wrote in Arabic, contributing to Islamic scholarship, but they also preserved and developed Persian literary traditions.

The translation movement in Baghdad, which brought Greek, Persian, and Indian texts into Arabic, relied heavily on Persian scholars and translators. Persian intellectual traditions thus became embedded in Islamic civilization.

Scientific and Intellectual Contributions

Persian scholars made fundamental contributions to the Islamic Golden Age. They advanced mathematics, astronomy, medicine, and philosophy, often building on both Greek and Persian knowledge traditions.

The House of Wisdom in Baghdad, a great center of learning, employed numerous Persian scholars. Their work in preserving ancient knowledge and advancing new discoveries helped make Baghdad the intellectual capital of the medieval world.

Cultural Resistance and Adaptation

Persian cultural survival under Islamic rule involved both resistance to assimilation and creative adaptation to new circumstances.

Preserving Persian Identity

Despite conversion to Islam, Persians maintained distinct cultural markers. The Persian language survived and eventually flourished, with New Persian emerging as a literary language. Persian festivals like Nowruz (New Year) continued to be celebrated, gradually being incorporated into Islamic cultural practice.

Persian historical memory remained strong. Scholars preserved stories of pre-Islamic Persian kings and heroes, maintaining connection to the Sasanian past even while participating fully in Islamic civilization.

Religious Adaptation

While many Persians converted to Islam, they often interpreted Islamic teachings through Persian cultural lenses. Some gravitated toward Shi'a Islam, which emphasized justice and the rights of the oppressed – themes that resonated with Persian political frustrations.

Zoroastrianism survived in reduced form, with communities maintaining their faith despite social and economic pressures. These Zoroastrian communities preserved ancient Persian religious texts and traditions.

Cultural Synthesis

Rather than choosing between Persian and Islamic identities, many Persians created a synthesis. They became devout Muslims while maintaining Persian cultural practices, demonstrating that religious and cultural identities could coexist.

This synthesis enriched Islamic civilization, making it more diverse and sophisticated than a purely Arab culture could have been. Persian contributions in administration, literature, science, and art became inseparable from Islamic achievement.

The Path Forward

By the end of the Abbasid period, Persians had transformed their defeat into cultural victory. Though they had lost political independence in 651 CE, they had preserved their identity and become essential to the Islamic world. This pattern of cultural persistence despite political subordination would characterize Persian history for centuries, eventually leading to the emergence of new Persian states that combined Islamic faith with Persian cultural identity.

Common Misconceptions About Persian Life Under Islamic Rule

Misconception 1: Persians Completely Lost Their Culture After the Arab Conquest

Reality: Persian culture not only survived but eventually became dominant in many aspects of Islamic civilization. Language, literature, administrative practices, and cultural traditions persisted and flourished.

Misconception 2: All Persians Immediately Converted to Islam

Reality: Conversion was gradual, taking several centuries. Many Persians initially remained Zoroastrian, and conversion often occurred for practical rather than purely spiritual reasons. Zoroastrian communities survived throughout the Islamic period.

Misconception 3: The Abbasid Revolution Was Purely Arab

Reality: The Abbasid Revolution succeeded partly because of Persian and other non-Arab support. The movement explicitly opposed Arab supremacy and promised a more inclusive Islamic state.

Misconception 4: Persians Had No Political Power Under the Caliphates

Reality: While Persians didn't hold the caliphate itself, they wielded enormous political influence under the Abbasids as viziers, governors, and administrators. Some Persian families became more powerful than many Arab nobles.

Misconception 5: Islamic Civilization Was Purely Arab

Reality: Islamic civilization was multicultural from early on, with Persian contributions being fundamental to its development. The Islamic Golden Age resulted from a synthesis between Arab, Persian, Greek, and other traditions.

Quick Summary:

Key Takeaways

- **Umayyad rule (661-750 CE)** marginalized Persians politically despite their administrative expertise, creating widespread discontent among non-Arab Muslims.

- **The Abbasid Revolution of 750 CE** overthrew the Umayyads and established a more inclusive government that integrated Persians into positions of real power.

- **Persian administrative systems, court culture, and intellectual traditions** became foundational to Abbasid governance and the Islamic Golden Age centered in Baghdad.

- **Persians maintained their cultural identity** through language preservation, continued celebration of traditional festivals, and maintenance of historical memory.

- **Cultural synthesis rather than assimilation** characterized the Persian experience, as they became devout Muslims while preserving distinct Persian cultural practices.

- **The Islamic Golden Age** resulted from collaboration between Arab, Persian, and other cultures, with Persian scholars making crucial contributions to science, philosophy, and literature.

- **Political defeat did not mean cultural extinction**—Persians demonstrated that a people could lose sovereignty while maintaining and even expanding their cultural influence within a new political order.

Chapter 9
The Persian Renaissance

The centuries following the Arab conquest of Persia could have meant the end of Persian culture. Instead, they ignited a remarkable revival. Between the 8th and 14th centuries, Persian scholars, poets, and thinkers helped shape the Islamic Golden Age - a period of extraordinary achievements that reshaped human knowledge.

Persian intellectuals didn't just preserve the past; they transformed ancient Greek, Indian, and Chinese wisdom into something new. They invented algebra, revolutionized medicine, wrote enduring poetry, and built cities that became global centers of learning.

The Persian Renaissance represents more than academic achievement. It shows how a conquered people maintained their identity while contributing to a broader civilization. Persian became a language of literature and administration across vast territories. Persian cities drew scholars from all over the world, and Persian thinkers pondered existence, knowledge, and the natural world - questions that continue to resonate.

This chapter explores how Persia rose from political defeat to intellectual triumph. We will examine the scientific breakthroughs, literary masterpieces, the cities and scholars driving innovation, and how this cultural renaissance helped Persians reclaim and reshape their identity within the Islamic world.

Advances in Science and Knowledge

The Persian contribution to science during the Islamic Golden Age significantly changed how humans understood the natural world. Persian scholars didn't just translate ancient texts; they questioned, tested, and expanded them.

Mathematics and the Birth of Algebra

Al-Khwarizmi, working in 9th-century Baghdad, created the mathematical field now known as algebra. His name gave us the word "algorithm," and his systematic approach to solving equations laid groundwork that modern mathematics still uses. He synthesized Greek, Indian, and Persian methods into something entirely new.

His works introduced Hindu-Arabic numerals to the Islamic world and eventually to Europe, replacing the cumbersome Roman numeral system. This change enabled complex calculations and accelerated scientific progress across multiple fields.

Revolutionary Medicine

Avicenna (Ibn Sina) wrote "The Canon of Medicine" in the early 11th century, which became the standard medical textbook for over 600 years. Born in present-day Uzbekistan to a Persian family, Avicenna synthesized Greek medical knowledge with his own observations.

He described contagious diseases, explained how infections spread, and identified tuberculosis as infectious - insights not widely accepted in Europe for centuries. He also pioneered experimental medicine, insisting theories be tested through observation.

Understanding Light and Vision

Ibn al-Haytham revolutionized optics in the 11th century. He refuted the Greek theory that eyes emit light rays and proved, through experiments, that light enters the eye.

His "Book of Optics" introduced the scientific method as we know it today: hypothesizing, experimenting, and concluding from evidence. His work laid the foundation for European scientists like Roger Bacon and Johannes Kepler.

Astronomy and Observation

Persian astronomers created star catalogs, refined astrolabes, and challenged Greek models. They calculated the Earth's circumference accurately and documented celestial movements with precision unmatched in Europe until the Renaissance.

These advances enabled improved navigation, reliable agricultural calendars, and precise religious timekeeping. Persian observatories became centers where theory met practical application.

The Translation Movement

The massive translation effort centered in Baghdad's House of Wisdom depended on Persian scholars who translated Greek, Sanskrit, and Syriac texts into Arabic. Beyond translating, they added commentaries, corrections, and extensions based on new discoveries.

This collaborative scholarship allowed knowledge from various civilizations to combine and generate new insights on an unprecedented scale.

The Rise of Persian Literature and Poetry

While Persian scientists advanced human knowledge, Persian poets and writers created a rich literary tradition influencing cultures from Turkey to India for centuries.

The Revival of Persian Language

After the Arab conquest, Arabic initially dominated literature. But by the 9th and 10th centuries, Persian re-emerged as a literary language, distinct in vocabulary, grammar, and spirit.

This was not a rejection of Islam or Arabic. Instead, Persian writers fostered a bilingual culture where Arabic served religious and legal purposes, while Persian expressed poetry, history, and cultural identity.

Ferdowsi and the Shahnameh

The poet Ferdowsi completed the "Shahnameh" around 1010 CE, creating Persian literature's most influential work. This epic poem recounted Persian history from mythical origins through the Arab conquest.

Ferdowsi used pure Persian vocabulary, preserving legends and values in a form compatible with Islamic civilization. The "Shahnameh" became a cultural touchstone, and its heroes remain central to Persian identity today.

The Poetry of Mysticism and Love

Persian poets developed sophisticated forms exploring love, mysticism, and human existence. The ghazal became the dominant form, expressing complex emotions in structured verse.

Rumi, in the 13th century, created poetry transcending cultural boundaries. His mystical verses explored divine love through metaphors of human longing, making his work globally celebrated and translated.

Omar Khayyam, known in the West for his poetry, was also a brilliant mathematician and astronomer. His "Rubaiyat" questioned conventional wisdom and celebrated the present moment in memorable language.

Literary Forms and Innovation

Persian poets innovated by developing masnavi, qasida, and ghazal. These forms required extraordinary skill, conveying deep meaning within strict meter and rhyme schemes. The best Persian poetry operates on multiple levels, rewarding repeated reading and contemplation.

Cultural Impact Beyond Persia

Persian became a literary language in a vast region. In Mughal India, Ottoman Turkey, and Central Asia, educated people wrote poetry in Persian, creating a shared intellectual space linking diverse peoples and regions.

This literary renaissance gave Persians cultural prestige that transcended political power. Persian poetry remained the gold standard for literary achievement across the Islamic world.

Scholars, Cities, and Innovation

The Persian Renaissance emerged from cities that became intellectual centers and from scholars who built networks of learning across vast distances.

Baghdad: The Intellectual Capital

Baghdad under the Abbasid Caliphate became the primary center for Persian intellectual activity. The House of Wisdom attracted scholars from across the Islamic world, many of them Persian.

Persian administrators and scholars held influential positions in the Abbasid court, bringing skills and curiosity that fostered a flourishing scholarly environment.

Nishapur and the Eastern Centers

Nishapur became a major learning center where Omar Khayyam worked. Prominent theologians, poets, and scientists gathered there, creating a vibrant intellectual community.

Other Persian cities like Rayy, Isfahan, and Shiraz developed scholarly circles, competing for prestige by attracting famous scholars and building libraries and colleges.

The Madrasa System

The development of madrasas provided formal structures for knowledge transmission. Madrasas offered systematic curricula and regular instruction, becoming models for higher education.

The Nizamiyya madrasas taught Islamic law, theology, logic, mathematics, and philosophy, preserving knowledge across generations.

Networks of Scholars

Persian scholars traveled extensively, studying with multiple teachers and building networks that spanned continents. They debated philosophy, mathematics, and medicine, creating a community of learning that transcended political boundaries.

Patronage and Support

Intellectual achievement required support. Persian viziers, governors, and merchants patronized scholars, funding research and libraries.

This system benefited rulers who gained prestige from scholarship. Advances in astronomy, medicine, and other fields had practical applications that improved life and governance.

The Role of Libraries

Major libraries preserved knowledge, employing copyists and making texts available to scholars. The loss of these libraries represented catastrophic setbacks to accumulated knowledge.

The Rebirth of Persian Identity

The Persian Renaissance was about more than science and poetry; it represented the rebirth of Persian identity within a changed world.

Cultural Survival Through Adaptation

After the Arab conquest, Persians creatively adapted to maintain cultural identity within an Islamic civilization.

Persian scholars mastered Arabic while reviving Persian language and literature. They embraced Islam while preserving Persian history and values, forming a dual identity that built renewed cultural confidence.

Language as Identity Marker

Reviving Persian as a literary language was crucial. Writing in Persian connected contemporary Persians to their pre-Islamic ancestors and created new literary and intellectual traditions.

Reinterpreting History

Persian writers reinterpreted history for the Islamic age. The "Shahnameh" presented pre-Islamic Persian kings as noble and wise, allowing Persians to honor their past within an Islamic present.

Administrative and Political Influence

Persian bureaucratic traditions shaped Islamic governance. Persian viziers wielded enormous influence, effectively running empires under caliphs.

This administrative role demonstrated that Persian civilization offered valuable knowledge and skills.

Cultural Prestige Across Regions

By the height of the Persian Renaissance, Persian culture commanded respect across vast regions. Turkish, Mongol, and Indian rulers adopted Persian as their court language and patronized Persian poets.

Persian culture shaped how empires expressed themselves, with poetry, administrative practices, and artistic styles marking sophistication and legitimacy.

Legacy of the Renaissance

The Persian Renaissance created enduring achievements. Even after the Mongol invasions devastated Persian cities, Persian culture survived by embedding itself deeply in Islamic civilization.

Common Misconceptions About the Persian Renaissance

Misconception 1: "The Islamic Golden Age was Arab, not Persian"

Reality: The Islamic Golden Age was multicultural, with many leading scholars being Persian, contributing significantly to its achievements.

Misconception 2: "Persian culture disappeared after the Arab conquest"

Reality: Persian culture adapted and flourished within Islamic civilization, becoming influential across vast territories.

Misconception 3: "Medieval Islamic science was just preservation of Greek knowledge"

Reality: Scholars like Al-Khwarizmi, Avicenna, and Ibn al-Haytham conducted original research and created new fields like algebra.

Misconception 4: "The Persian Renaissance was anti-Islamic"

Reality: The Persian Renaissance occurred within Islamic civilization, with scholars who were devout Muslims and saw no conflict with Persian cultural pride.

Misconception 5: "This period's achievements had no impact on Europe"

Reality: European advancements in science and medicine built on Islamic Golden Age achievements, including Persian contributions to mathematics and medicine.

Quick Summary

Key Takeaways:

- The Islamic Golden Age (8th-14th centuries) saw Persian scholars revolutionize science, mathematics, medicine, and astronomy.

- Al-Khwarizmi created algebra and introduced numerals; Avicenna's medical texts were used for centuries; Ibn al-Haytham pioneered the scientific method.

- Persian literature flourished, with Ferdowsi's "Shahnameh" preserving history and identity, and Persian poetry becoming the literary standard.

- Cities like Baghdad and Nishapur became intellectual centers where scholars collaborated.

- The madrasa system formalized education, preserving knowledge across generations.

- Persians maintained identity by adapting to Islamic civilization and reviving Persian language and literature.

- Persian culture commanded respect beyond political borders, influencing regions from Turkey to India.

- The Persian Renaissance demonstrated how cultural and intellectual achievement could reshape the civilization of conquerors.

PART 4
THE MAKING OF MODERN IRAN

Chapter 10
The Safavid Revolution

The year 1501 marked a turning point in Persian history. When a young warrior named Shah Ismail captured the city of Tabriz, he launched a revolution that would reshape the region's identity. The Safavid Dynasty he founded transformed Persia into Iran, established Shi'a Islam as a defining feature of Iranian identity, and created a centralized state that would influence the Middle East for centuries.

This chapter explores how the Safavids emerged from a religious movement to build an empire. It examines Shah Ismail's rise to power, the religious transformation he imposed, the administrative systems that held his empire together, and the lasting legacy of Safavid rule. Understanding this period is essential for comprehending modern Iran, the Sunni-Shi'a divide, and the political dynamics of the Middle East today.

The Safavid Revolution was not merely a change of rulers. It was a fundamental reimagining of Persian identity, religious practice, and political organization that continues to shape the region more than five centuries later.

The Rise of the Safavids

The Safavid Dynasty did not emerge from nowhere. Its roots lay in the Safaviyeh, a Sufi religious order in Azarbaijan. This mystical Islamic movement combined spiritual devotion with military discipline, attracting followers who were both believers and warriors.

From Spiritual Order to Military Power

The Safaviyeh order transformed from a peaceful religious community into a militant organization. Its followers, known as the Qezelbash ("red heads" for their distinctive turbans), became a formidable fighting force. They viewed their leaders not just as spiritual guides but as divinely appointed rulers worthy of absolute loyalty.

This combination of religious fervor and military capability proved explosive. The Qezelbash believed they were engaged in a holy mission rather than mere conquest.

Shah Ismail: The Young Conqueror

Shah Ismail I was only fourteen when he began his campaign to establish an empire. Despite his youth, he possessed remarkable charisma and military skill. In 1501, Ismail captured Tabriz, marking the official foundation of the Safavid Empire. From this base, he rapidly expanded his control across Persian territories.

Military Strategy and Expansion

The Qezelbash cavalry formed the backbone of Ismail's military success. These mounted warriors combined speed, discipline, and religious zeal, believing they were establishing God's kingdom on earth. Ismail's campaigns were swift and decisive, and within a decade, he had brought much of Persia under Safavid control.

A New Name for an Ancient Land

Shah Ismail made a symbolic decision reflecting his ambitions: he rechristened Persia as Iran. This was more than a name change; it represented an effort to connect his empire to Iran's ancient heritage while creating a distinct identity separate from the surrounding Sunni Muslim powers.

The rise of the Safavids demonstrated how religious movements could transform into political powers. But Ismail's most consequential decision was to make Shi'a Islam the official religion of his empire.

The Establishment of Shi'a Islam

Shah Ismail's declaration of Shi'a Islam as Iran's state religion was one of history's most dramatic transformations. This decision would permanently alter the Middle East's religious landscape and create a distinct Iranian identity.

A Revolutionary Religious Policy

When Ismail came to power, most of Persia's population practiced Sunni Islam. Ismail reversed this reality by declaring Shi'a Islam - specifically Twelver Shi'ism - as the only acceptable form of Islam, enforced by the state.

Methods of Conversion

The conversion was neither gentle nor gradual. Ismail employed multiple strategies:

- **Forced conversion**: Sunni Muslims were required to curse revered Sunni figures.

- **Importation of scholars**: Shi'a scholars were brought in to educate the population.

- **Persecution of resistance**: Refusal led to punishment or death.

- **Control of religious institutions**: Mosques and schools were placed under state supervision.

Political Motivations

Ismail's religious policy served clear political purposes. By making Iran distinctly Shi'a, he created a boundary between his empire and Sunni powers like the Ottoman Empire. This distinction fostered national unity, with Iran unified under Shi'a faith.

Long-Term Consequences

The establishment of Shi'a Islam as Iran's state religion had profound effects:

- **Permanent religious identity**: Iran remains predominantly Shi'a today.

- **Regional tensions**: The Sunni-Shi'a divide became a source of conflict.

- **Cultural distinctiveness**: Shi'a practices shaped Iranian culture.

- **Political legitimacy**: Future rulers derived legitimacy from their protection of Shi'a Islam.

Within generations, Iran's population largely embraced Shi'a identity, showing the power of state authority to reshape religious practice.

Building a Centralized State

Religious transformation alone could not sustain an empire. Shah Ismail and his successors needed effective administrative systems to govern their territories.

The Challenge of Ethnic Diversity

The Safavid Empire faced a tension between the Turkish-speaking Qezelbash military and Persian bureaucrats. Managing this tension became a constant challenge.

Administrative Structure

The Safavids developed a centralized government:

- **The Shah**: Absolute authority rested with the monarch.

- **Provincial governors**: Appointed officials administered regions.

- **Bureaucratic offices**: Persian administrators handled governance.

- **Religious establishment**: Shi'a clergy gained state support.

Economic Prosperity

The Safavid state promoted economic development. Trade routes connected East and West, bolstering trade and commercial prosperity. Infrastructure investments supported agriculture and urban growth.

Social Welfare and Cultural Development

Safavid rulers sponsored architectural projects, educational institutions, and artisans, creating a distinctive culture blending Persian traditions with Shi'a themes.

International Relations

The Safavid period saw increased engagement with foreign powers. European states sought alliances, bringing new technologies and trade opportunities.

A Lasting Transformation

Safavid mosque interior (Shah Mosque, Isfahan)

The Safavid Dynasty ruled Iran from 1501 to 1736. When the empire collapsed, it left a transformed society whose characteristics persist today.

National Unity Through Religion

The Safavids forged a unified Iranian identity by making Shi'a Islam a defining feature. This religious nationalism proved durable, even after the dynasty ended.

Cultural Renaissance

The Safavid period witnessed a flourishing of Persian culture. Isfahan's architecture still attracts visitors, and Persian literature and crafts reached new heights.

The Sunni-Shi'a Divide

The establishment of Shi'a Islam permanently altered the Middle East's religious geography, influencing regional politics.

Administrative Legacy

The Safavid model of centralized government influenced subsequent Iranian states, with a partnership between monarchy and clergy becoming defining.

Limitations and Decline

The Safavid system faced internal tensions and external pressures, leading to its collapse. Yet its core achievements survived.

Modern Relevance

Understanding the Safavid Revolution is essential for comprehending modern Iran, its religious character, regional relations, and political systems.

Common Misconceptions About the Safavid Revolution

Misconception 1: The Safavids were Persian

The Safavid Dynasty had Turkish origins. The Qezelbash warriors were Turkmen, but they adopted Persian as the administrative language.

Misconception 2: Iran was always Shi'a

Before the Safavids, most of Persia practiced Sunni Islam. The conversion to Shi'a Islam was a state-imposed transformation.

Misconception 3: The religious conversion was peaceful

The establishment of Shi'a Islam involved coercion and forced conversion.

Misconception 4: The Safavid Empire was isolated

The period saw increased international engagement with European missions and cultural exchanges.

Misconception 5: The Safavid legacy ended in 1736

While the dynasty collapsed, its legacies - Shi'a identity and Iranian unity - continued to shape Iran.

Quick Summary:

Key Takeaways

- **Shah Ismail I founded the Safavid Dynasty in 1501** by capturing Tabriz and establishing control over Persian territories.

- **The Safavids transformed Iran's religious identity** by instituting Shi'a Islam as the state religion.

- **Religious transformation served political purposes**, creating a distinctive Iranian identity.

- **The empire balanced Turkish military power with Persian administrative expertise**, managing internal tensions.

- **Safavid rule promoted economic prosperity and cultural development**, creating a flourishing civilization.

- **The dynasty lasted until 1736**, but its legacy continues to shape the region today.

- **The Safavid Revolution altered the Middle East's religious geography**, influencing regional politics.

- **Understanding the Safavid period is crucial for comprehending modern Iran**, its religious character, regional relationships, and political systems.

Chapter 11
A Nation Between Empires

The Safavid Empire's survival hinged on deft maneuvering within a volatile geopolitical sphere. Wedged between the mighty Ottoman Empire to the west and new threats emerging from Central Asia, Persia faced relentless military pressure in the late 16th and early 17th centuries. Yet, this era was marked not solely by warfare. Under visionary leaders, particularly Shah Abbas I, the Safavids turned military challenges into opportunities for diplomatic innovation, administrative reform, and cultural flourishing.

This chapter explores how Persia maintained its independence and identity amidst imperial rivalries, examining the Ottoman conflicts that shaped its borders, the internal reforms that solidified its governance, and the cultural achievements that flourished despite - or perhaps due to - these challenges.

Conflict with the Ottoman Empire

The First Ottoman-Safavid War (1578-1590)

The late 16th century placed Persia in a precarious position. The Ottoman Empire, under aggressive leadership, launched a major offensive against Safavid territories in 1578, driven by both territorial ambitions and deep religious divisions. The Sunni Ottomans viewed the Shia Safavids as heretics, while the Safavids saw themselves as the defenders of true Islam.

The war was devastating for Persia, with better-equipped Ottoman forces advancing deep into Safavid lands. By 1590, the Treaty of Istanbul forced the Safavids to cede significant territories, including parts of the Caucasus and western Persia - a humiliating setback for the young Safavid state.

Shah Abbas I's Strategic Recovery

The ascension of Shah Abbas I in 1588 marked a turning point. Realizing that immediate military parity with the Ottomans was unrealistic, Abbas focused on rebuilding the army and reforming state governance. He established a standing army loyal directly to the crown, reducing reliance on tribal forces.

By launching a recovery campaign in 1603, Abbas's reformed military proved superior. Through strategic campaigns and diplomacy, he systematically reclaimed territories. His forces exhibited tactical sophistication, using mobile cavalry effectively and developing improved artillery.

The Second Treaty of Istanbul in 1612 formalized these gains, restoring crucial regions to Safavid control and reestablishing Persian prestige and power.

The Georgian Question and Baghdad Conflicts

The Caucasus, especially Georgia, remained a focal point of contention. Its strategic location prompted repeated conflicts, leading to the Treaty of Srao in 1618, which, despite failing to prevent future disputes, provided temporary stability.

Baghdad was another flashpoint. In 1622, a conflict over this significant city erupted. Beyond military strategy, Baghdad held cultural and religious importance for both empires. The Safavid acquisition of Baghdad was a notable victory, even as Ottoman efforts to retake it continued to strain relations.

The Pattern of Conflict and Diplomacy

The Ottoman-Safavid conflicts followed a pattern of intense military campaigns alternated with diplomatic truces. These periods allowed both empires to consolidate gains and rebuild. Periodic truces were necessary as neither side possessed resources for sustained total war.

Shah Abbas I skillfully cultivated European allies to counterbalance Ottoman power, opening strategic trade routes and accessing European military technology and expertise.

Internal Stability and Governance

Administrative Reforms Under Abbas I

Shah Abbas I understood that military success required a stable state. He implemented comprehensive administrative reforms, replacing the traditional system reliant on autonomous tribal leaders with a more centralized structure.

Abbas created administrative positions staffed by officials loyal to the crown. He established a systematic tax collection, reducing corruption and increasing efficiency, crucial for financing campaigns and public projects.

Reforming the military, he established a standing army of ghulams - slave soldiers loyal to him. This force ensured military reliability, vital for external and internal stability.

Balancing Power and Loyalty

Stability required managing power centers. Abbas skillfully balanced the influential Qizilbash tribes, crucial in establishing Safavid power, rewarding loyalty while reducing their autonomy.

Promoting capable individuals regardless of ethnicity created a meritocratic system, broadening support for the regime. Regular rotation of provincial governors prevented them from amassing independent power bases.

Economic Foundations of Stability

Economic prosperity underpinned political stability. Abbas invested in infrastructure, enhancing trade routes and developing the silk trade, a major revenue and diplomatic tool.

By fostering direct trade with Europe, Persia circumvented Ottoman routes, boosting silk profits. European merchants also brought technical knowledge and diplomatic connections.

Religious Authority and State Power

The Shia identity was central to Safavid legitimacy. Abbas maintained close ties with religious scholars, ensuring their support for royal authority. He funded religious institutions, creating a mutually beneficial relationship that strengthened state legitimacy.

Religious scholars played roles in administration, particularly in family law and property disputes, integrating religious and political authorities.

Urban Development and Social Order

Abbas relocated the capital to Isfahan, transforming it into a symbol of stability and ambition. Isfahan's development attracted merchants, artisans, and demonstrated governmental capacity for grand projects.

Urban development extended to provincial cities, improving quality of life and demonstrating government commitment to welfare, boosting popular support.

Cultural and Artistic Growth

Isfahan: The Jewel of Persia

Isfahan's transformation into the capital was a monumental achievement. Shah Abbas I envisioned it as a showcase of Persian culture and power, resulting in a meticulously planned city with magnificent architecture and infrastructure.

Naqsh-e Jahan Square, a massive public space surrounded by architectural marvels, became the city's centerpiece. Its design blended Persian aesthetics with practical functions.

Isfahan's bridges combined engineering excellence with artistic beauty, while its gardens followed traditional Persian designs, offering residents green sanctuaries.

Architectural Innovation

Safavid architecture reached new heights, blending Persian traditions with new elements. The use of intricate tilework produced stunning geometric and floral patterns.

Mosque design evolved, with architects perfecting double-shell domes for impressive interiors. The Shah Mosque exemplifies this, its dome seemingly floating above the prayer hall.

Caravanserais served as essential infrastructure for trade, melding functionality with beauty and reinforcing the state's commitment to commerce.

The Flourishing of Persian Arts

Miniature painting achieved extraordinary refinement, with artists developing techniques for incredible detail and color. These works illustrated literature and court life, serving as art and historical records.

Calligraphy flourished, with master calligraphers enjoying court prestige. Their integration into architecture created a distinctive aesthetic for religious texts and proclamations.

Carpet weaving became an art form, with Persian carpets from this era among history's finest. Complex patterns and quality materials made them prized internationally, economically essential for Persia.

Literary and Intellectual Life

The Safavid court patronized poets, historians, and scholars, supporting Persian literary traditions while encouraging innovation. Chronicles documented the period, providing insight into Safavid society.

Poetry was central. Poets, drawing on classical traditions, addressed contemporary themes and celebrated royal achievements, shaping culture.

Intellectual exchanges with the Islamic world and Europe enriched Persian cultural life, encouraging creativity and keeping scholarship connected to broader developments.

Cultural Diplomacy

Cultural accomplishments served diplomatic purposes. Foreign visitors to Isfahan left impressed by Persian sophistication, spreading its reputation abroad. Artistic gifts showcased Persian craftsmanship and refinement.

Welcoming foreign artists created a cosmopolitan culture, enriching Persian arts and demonstrating the empire's confidence. European travelers' accounts shaped perceptions of Persia as refined and civilized.

Common Misconceptions About Safavid Persia

Misconception: The Ottoman-Safavid conflicts were purely religious wars.

While religious differences intensified conflicts, territorial and strategic interests were equally important. Both empires sought control of trade routes and resources.

Misconception: Persia was constantly at war during this period.

Conflicts followed a pattern of intense campaigns followed by extended truces. Treaties in 1590, 1612, and 1618 allowed for internal development.

Misconception: Shah Abbas I was merely a military leader.

Abbas's legacy includes significant administrative reforms, diplomatic initiatives, and cultural patronage. He was a sophisticated statesman who understood the need for more than military strength.

Misconception: Safavid cultural achievements were isolated from broader Islamic culture.

Persian culture remained connected to broader Islamic artistic and intellectual traditions, engaging with global developments.

Misconception: The centralization of power eliminated all regional autonomy.

Abbas reduced tribal chiefs' power but maintained regional governance, balancing central authority with traditional structures.

Quick Summary

Key Takeaways:

- The Ottoman-Safavid conflicts (1578-1622) alternated between warfare and diplomacy, with neither empire achieving lasting dominance.

- Shah Abbas I revitalized Safavid fortunes through military reforms, creating a standing army loyal to the crown.

- The Treaty of Istanbul (1612) restored Persian territories, enhancing Safavid prestige and regional influence.

- Administrative centralization under Abbas I improved governance while balancing traditional power structures.

- Economic prosperity from the silk trade and European diplomacy financed military campaigns and public works.

- Isfahan's transformation into a cultural capital demonstrated Safavid sophistication and aided in cultural diplomacy.

- Persian arts, including architecture, miniature painting, calligraphy, and carpet weaving, reached exceptional refinement.

- Cultural achievements were intertwined with political realities, serving diplomatic purposes and reflecting the empire's resilience.

Chapter 12
Decline and Foreign Control

The nineteenth century marked a turning point for Afghanistan. As internal leadership weakened and rival factions vied for power, two expanding empires - Russia and Great Britain - focused on Central Asia.

Caught between these forces, Afghanistan became a central player in "The Great Game," a struggle for influence and control. This chapter examines how governance weaknesses, external pressure, and geopolitical competition eroded Afghan sovereignty.

We explore foreign intervention mechanisms, economic and military pressures from imperial powers, and how Afghanistan's strategic location became a vulnerability. By the end of this chapter, you'll understand how an independent nation became a buffer state manipulated by foreign interests.

Weak Leadership and Instability

Afghanistan entered the nineteenth century politically fragmented. The centralized authority of earlier periods crumbled as regional leaders, tribal chiefs, and royal factions contested for power.

The Collapse of Central Authority

Without strong leadership, the government struggled to maintain basic functions. Tax collection faltered. Military forces answered local commanders rather than a central authority. Provincial governors acted independently, forming alliances and making decisions without coordinating with Kabul.

This internal weakness created a power vacuum. Regional strongmen filled the void, each controlling territories through personal loyalties rather than institutional governance, resulting in a patchwork of competing authorities.

Succession Crises and Civil Conflict

Leadership transitions often led to violence. Multiple claimants emerged when rulers died, each backed by different tribal coalitions. These disputes frequently escalated into conflict, draining resources and weakening state capacity.

Instability hindered long-term planning. Infrastructure projects stalled, and trade routes became hazardous. Foreign merchants and diplomats viewed Afghanistan as unreliable.

Vulnerability to External Pressure

Internal chaos made Afghanistan vulnerable to foreign manipulation. Weak leaders sought external support, often making concessions that compromised sovereignty. Foreign powers exploited this vulnerability systematically.

The stage was set for unprecedented outside intervention.

Russian Expansion into the Region

Throughout the nineteenth century, Russia pursued aggressive southward expansion into Central Asia. This movement brought Russian forces closer to Afghanistan's northern borders, altering the regional power balance.

The Southward Push

Russia's expansion was relentless. Forces moved through Central Asia, conquering khanates and establishing military outposts. Cities like Tashkent, Samarkand, and Bukhara fell under Russian control, bringing the empire's frontier to Afghanistan's doorstep.

Russia sought warm-water ports, new markets, and strategic depth. Central Asia offered all these, plus valuable cotton production to reduce dependence on American imports.

Strategic Objectives

Russia's interest in Afghanistan was geopolitical. A foothold there provided access to the Indian subcontinent and threatened British interests. Russian influence in Afghanistan could disrupt British trade routes without direct conquest.

Russian diplomats established contacts with Afghan leaders, offering military support and financial assistance, providing Russia leverage over Afghan internal affairs without military occupation.

Military Capabilities and Presence

Russian military technology and organization far surpassed Afghanistan's fragmented forces. Modern artillery and disciplined infantry enabled power projection across vast distances. Afghan leaders realized direct confrontation with Russia likely meant defeat.

Russian military posts along Afghanistan's northern frontier were constant reminders of this power imbalance, influencing every major Afghan political decision.

Impact on Afghan Politics

Some Afghan leaders saw Russia as an ally against British pressure. Others viewed Russian expansion as a threat. This division created internal conflict, with pro-Russian and anti-Russian factions vying for influence.

The Russian presence forced Afghan leaders to navigate between two empires rather than pursue independent policies.

British Influence and Economic Pressure

While Russia expanded from the north, Great Britain tightened its grip from the south. British India shared a long border with Afghanistan, and maintaining Afghan stability was viewed as essential to protecting this colonial possession.

The Great Game Begins

The rivalry between Russia and Britain became known as "The Great Game," capturing the strategic, often covert nature of their competition. Afghanistan stood at the center, a buffer state whose alignment could tip the balance.

British officials feared Russian influence would threaten India's security, believing Russian agents operating from Afghanistan could incite rebellion or provide a staging ground for invasion.

Economic Leverage

Britain wielded economic power as a primary tool. British India controlled Afghanistan's main trade routes, and Afghan merchants depended on access to Indian markets and British-controlled ports.

Britain used this economic dependency strategically. Trade agreements included political conditions, with tariffs adjusted to reward or punish Afghan leaders. British subsidies created financial dependence that translated into political influence.

The U.S. Civil War strengthened Britain's position by disrupting global cotton supplies, increasing regional trade leverage.

Military and Diplomatic Pressure

British India maintained a formidable military presence along Afghanistan's borders, making clear they would intervene to prevent Russian dominance. This credible threat was paired with efforts to install friendly rulers in Kabul and prevent alliances with Russia.

Surveillance and Intelligence

British intelligence networks penetrated Afghan politics deeply. Agents and informants provided detailed information, enabling Britain to respond swiftly to threats and opportunities.

The combination of economic control, military capability, and superior intelligence made British influence difficult to resist.

The Loss of Sovereignty

By the late nineteenth century, Afghanistan had lost control over its destiny, caught between Russian and British pressures.

The Buffer State Reality

Afghanistan evolved from an independent nation to a buffer state - a territory primarily serving to separate rival empires. Both Russia and Britain preferred a weak Afghanistan that could stabilize the region without asserting independence.

Afghan sovereignty existed more in theory than practice. Major policy decisions needed consideration of British and Russian reactions.

Constrained Decision-Making

Afghan rulers faced impossible choices. Aligning with Russia risked British intervention; accepting British demands invited Russian pressure. Playing both sides satisfied neither.

The loss of sovereignty was gradual but comprehensive. Foreign advisors influenced military organization and trade policies, even requiring approval for internal security arrangements.

Economic Dependency

Afghanistan's economy depended heavily on foreign support. British subsidies funded government operations, and market access determined merchant prosperity, reinforcing political subordination.

Leaders attempting independence found themselves isolated and economically strangled, with foreign control undeniable.

Long-Term Consequences

The sovereignty loss during this period established patterns persisting for generations. Afghanistan's identity as a buffer state and its vulnerability to foreign manipulation originated in this era.

The geopolitical competition transformed Afghanistan from a regional power into contested territory, shaping its history well into the twentieth century and beyond.

Common Misconceptions

Misconception 1: Afghanistan was formally colonized like India

Afghanistan never became a formal colony. Instead, it was a buffer state with nominal independence but heavy foreign influence.

Misconception 2: The Great Game was primarily military

While military threats were important, the Great Game relied on economic pressure, diplomatic manipulation, and intelligence operations.

Misconception 3: Afghan leaders were passive victims

Afghan rulers actively attempted to manipulate the Russia-Britain rivalry, extracting temporary concessions despite the overall trend of foreign control.

Misconception 4: Internal weakness solely led to foreign control

While internal instability allowed foreign intervention, Russia's and Britain's overwhelming power would have exerted pressure regardless.

Misconception 5: The loss of sovereignty was sudden

The erosion of sovereignty was gradual, occurring over decades through accumulated concessions and dependencies.

Quick Summary

Key Takeaways:

- **Internal fragmentation** due to weak leadership made Afghanistan vulnerable

- **Russian expansion** in Central Asia brought a powerful threat with superior military capabilities

- **The Great Game** transformed Afghanistan into a buffer state

- **British economic leverage** created dependencies that translated into political influence

- **Loss of sovereignty** happened gradually, with constrained Afghan policy options

- **Buffer state status** served great powers as a barrier, not as an independent nation

- **Economic dependency** reinforced political subordination

- **Long-term intervention** patterns were established, influencing modern Afghan history

Chapter 13
Life in Iran Before Modernity

The Safavid period (1501-1736) marks a transformative era in Iranian history. Led by Shah Ismail I and his successors, Iran underwent profound changes in religious identity, social organization, and economic life. This chapter delves into the daily existence of ordinary Iranians during this pivotal period - before the advent of modern technologies and global influences that would later reshape the country.

Understanding pre-modern Iranian life requires looking beyond royal courts and military campaigns. Daily rhythms were shaped by religious practices, social hierarchies, economic activities, and cultural traditions. While the Safavid rulers established Twelver Shi'ism as the state religion and unified the Iranian plateau, the lived experiences of merchants, craftsmen, farmers, and religious scholars reveal a society balancing tradition with gradual change.

This chapter examines four key dimensions of pre-modern Iranian life: the social structures organizing communities, the religious influences on daily routines, the economic systems sustaining populations, and the cultural practices defining Iranian identity. Through these elements, we gain insight into how people navigated their world during a time bridging medieval traditions and modern Iran's foundations.

Social Structure and Daily Life

Pre-modern Iranian society was hierarchically structured. At the top were the Shah and the royal court, followed by religious scholars (ulama), government officials, and military commanders. Beneath them were urban merchants and craftsmen, with farmers and rural laborers forming the social base.

Urban Life

Cities like Isfahan, Tabriz, and Qazvin were centers of commerce, religion, and culture. Residents lived in neighborhoods often organized by profession or religious affiliation. Wealthy merchants and officials resided in spacious homes, while craftsmen and laborers occupied modest quarters near workshops or markets.

Daily routines revolved around prayer times, market hours, and seasonal patterns. Men typically worked in bazaars or offices, while women managed households, some engaging in textile production or trade. Public bathhouses (hammams) were vital social spaces for gathering, news exchange, and hygiene.

Rural Life

Most Iranians lived in rural areas as farmers, herders, or village craftsmen. Life followed agricultural cycles - planting, harvesting, and managing qanats (irrigation systems) that brought water from underground to fields and settlements.

Village life centered on extended families and tribal affiliations. Landowners or local chiefs held authority, collecting taxes and mediating disputes. Communities upheld traditions of hospitality and mutual assistance, crucial for survival in harsh environments.

Social Mobility

Though social hierarchies were rigid, some mobility existed. Individuals could rise through religious education, military service, or successful trade. The Safavid emphasis on Shi'ism opened avenues for religious scholars to gain influence and wealth through positions in mosques, courts, and educational institutions.

Religion in Everyday Society

The establishment of Twelver Shi'ism as the state religion under the Safavids fundamentally shaped daily life. This religious shift, initiated by Shah Ismail I in 1501, restructured social relationships, cultural practices, and individual routines.

Daily Religious Practice

Five daily prayers punctuated each day. Mosques were centers for worship, education, and community gatherings. The call to prayer (adhan) reminded believers of religious duties, influencing hygiene, dietary practices, and social interactions.

Religious observances extended beyond prayer. Fasting during Ramadan united communities in spiritual discipline. Charitable giving (zakat) supported the needy and funded religious institutions. Pilgrimages to holy sites like Mashhad and Qom were significant spiritual journeys.

The Role of Religious Scholars

Ulama wielded significant influence, interpreting religious law (sharia), resolving disputes, overseeing marriages, and providing education. Their authority extended to commerce, family relations, and community governance.

Religious schools (madrasas) trained scholars and provided basic education, preserving knowledge and serving as intellectual centers.

Shi'ite Distinctiveness

Twelver Shi'ism introduced practices distinguishing Iranian religious life. Commemorating Imam Hussein's martyrdom at Karbala was central to religious identity. Mourning ceremonies during Muharram reinforced communal bonds and devotion.

Trade, Economy, and Craftsmanship

The economy of pre-modern Iran relied on agriculture, craft production, and long-distance trade. Safavid political consolidation fostered economic growth and cultural exchange across a vast territory.

The Bazaar System

Bazaars were the economic heart of cities. Merchants and craftsmen were organized by specialty - each occupying designated sections. Guilds (asnaf) regulated quality, prices, and training.

Bazaars were also social centers for news exchange, partnerships, and discussions. Wealthy merchants often funded religious institutions and public works, gaining prestige.

Craft Production

Iranian craftsmen were internationally recognized. Carpet weaving, especially in Kashan and Kerman, produced intricate designs prized globally. Metalworkers created elaborate vessels and weapons. Ceramic production, manuscript illumination, and textile dyeing were crafts passed down through generations.

Workshops operated on apprenticeship systems, preserving traditional knowledge while allowing innovation.

Trade Networks

Iran's geographic position made it a crucial link in trade routes. Caravans transported silk, spices, and other goods across the territory. Caravanserais offered rest and security along major routes.

Armenian merchants played key roles, connecting Iranian markets with European, Indian, and Central Asian centers.

Traditions and Cultural Practices

Pre-modern Iranian cultural identity reflected layers of tradition. While Shi'ism reshaped religious practice, many cultural traditions predated Islam and defined Iranian distinctiveness.

Nowruz and Seasonal Celebrations

Nowruz, the Persian New Year, remained the most important festival. Families prepared special foods, cleaned homes, and gathered for celebrations blending pre-Islamic traditions with Islamic practices. The haft-sin table connected ancient customs to religious contexts.

Other celebrations marked agricultural cycles and religious observances, strengthening community bonds.

Family and Gender Roles

Extended families were the basic social units. Patriarchal authority governed decisions, though women exerted influence within households. Marriage arrangements involved family negotiations considering status and alliances.

Women's public roles varied by class and location. Elite women wielded political influence, while rural women participated in agricultural work. Urban women typically maintained strict separation from unrelated men.

Arts and Literature

Persian poetry was central to cultural life. Works by poets like Hafez, Rumi, and Saadi were memorized and discussed across classes. Poetry provided entertainment, moral instruction, and spiritual guidance.

Music accompanied celebrations and ceremonies. Storytelling traditions preserved historical narratives. Visual arts like miniature painting and calligraphy adorned manuscripts and architecture.

Hospitality and Social Customs

Hospitality (mehman-navazi) was highly valued. Guests were received with elaborate rituals. Tea houses (chaikhanehs) served as male social spaces for tea, conversation, and business.

Common Misconceptions About Pre-Modern Iranian Life

Misconception 1: Pre-modern Iran was uniformly poor and backward

Reality: Safavid Iran had prosperous cities, sophisticated crafts, and extensive trade networks, with Iranian goods commanding high international prices.

Misconception 2: Religion completely dominated every aspect of life

Reality: While Shi'ism was central, Iranians maintained traditions like Nowruz, blending religious and secular activities.

Misconception 3: Women had no social roles or influence

Reality: Women managed households, engaged in production, influenced decisions, and occasionally wielded power, with experiences varying by class and location.

Misconception 4: Iranian society was completely isolated

Reality: Iran's position on trade routes ensured constant contact with various cultures, facilitated by merchant communities.

Misconception 5: Daily life remained unchanged

Reality: The Safavid period featured significant transformations in religion and politics, with urban growth, trade expansion, and cultural developments altering life.

Quick Summary

Key Takeaways:

- Iranian society had clear hierarchies with defined roles for Shah, religious scholars, merchants, craftsmen, and farmers.

- Urban life centered on bazaars and mosques while rural communities followed agricultural cycles.

- Twelver Shi'ism reshaped daily routines and cultural practices.

- Religious scholars played a central role in governance and education.

- The economy relied on agriculture, crafts, and trade.

- Cultural traditions blended Islamic and pre-Islamic customs, evident in celebrations like Nowruz.

- Family structures, gender roles, and artistic traditions defined cultural identity.

PART 5
OIL, POWER, AND REVOLUTION

Chapter 14
The Rise of the Shah

The early twentieth century marked a turning point in Iranian history. After centuries of dynastic rule under the Qājārs, Iran faced a choice between tradition and modernity. The Constitutional Revolution of 1906 had promised reform and representative government, yet political instability and foreign interference persisted. From this turmoil emerged a military officer poised to reshape Iran's future: Reza Khan, who would become Reza Shah Pahlavi and establish a new dynasty focused on rapid modernization.

This chapter explores the rise of the Pahlavi dynasty and its ambitious - but controversial - transformation of Iran. We examine how Reza Shah seized power, the sweeping reforms he implemented, and the complex interplay between modernization and Western influence that would shape Iran for decades. Understanding this era is crucial to comprehending modern Iranian history, as its successes and failures directly influenced the revolutionary movements that eventually overthrew the monarchy in 1979.

The Rise of Reza Shah

The End of the Qājār Dynasty

By 1921, Iran confronted a crisis of legitimacy and sovereignty. The Qājār Dynasty, ruling since 1789, struggled to resist foreign encroachment or implement reforms. The Constitutional Revolution of 1906 forced the establishment of a constitutional monarchy and Iran's first parliament, but representative government remained unfulfilled.

Foreign powers, mainly Britain and Russia, wielded significant influence over Iran. The economy was weak, the military ineffective, and the central government lacked control over much of the territory.

Regional warlords and tribal leaders operated with near autonomy, while foreign troops occupied Iranian soil.

Reza Khan's Coup

Into this vacuum stepped Reza Khan, a military officer risen through the Cossack Brigade ranks. On February 21, 1921, he led a bloodless coup, effectively ending Qājār rule, though the last shah did not formally abdicate until 1925.

Reza Khan initially served as Minister of War and later as Prime Minister. He skillfully consolidated power while maintaining constitutional legitimacy. He eliminated rival power centers, bringing regional strongmen under control and building a national army.

Establishing the Pahlavi Dynasty

In 1926, Reza Khan became Reza Shah Pahlavi, founding a new dynasty. The name "Pahlavi" referenced the Middle Persian language, linking the regime to Iran's pre-Islamic past and emphasizing Persian nationalism.

Reza Shah envisioned a transformation inspired by the modernization programs of Atatürk in Turkey and Peter the Great in Russia. Unlike previous gradual reforms, he pursued rapid, top-down modernization affecting all aspects of Iranian life.

Consolidating Power

Reza Shah moved swiftly to centralize authority. He subdued tribal confederations, brought the clergy under state control, and established an efficient bureaucracy. His authoritarian methods tolerated little opposition, using the military and security forces to enforce compliance.

He sought to reduce foreign influence, a complicated goal. While limiting British and Soviet interference, his modernization increased reliance on Western technology, expertise, and economic models.

Modernization and Reform

Infrastructure and Industrialization

Reza Shah initiated a program to modernize Iran's infrastructure, knowing economic development required reliable transportation and communication.

Key projects included:

- The Trans-Iranian Railway (completed 1938), linking the Persian Gulf to the Caspian Sea

- Development of roads between major cities

- Establishment of modern ports

- Creation of telegraph and postal systems

- Construction of modern hospitals and clinics

The Trans-Iranian Railway, built without foreign loans, symbolized Iranian independence and capability. It also served strategic purposes, extending government control.

Reza Shah promoted industrialization through state-sponsored factories and protective tariffs. New industries included textiles, cement, sugar refineries, and tobacco processing. Despite these efforts, Iran remained primarily agricultural and dependent on oil revenues.

Educational and Legal Reforms

Education became central to modernization. Reza Shah established Tehran University in 1934 and expanded public education, founding secular schools and sending students abroad.

The legal system underwent transformation. Reza Shah replaced religious courts with secular civil courts based on European models, reducing the clergy's judicial authority and challenging traditional power structures.

Social and Cultural Changes

Reza Shah controversially sought to reshape society and culture:

Dress codes: In 1928, he mandated Western-style dress for men, banning traditional garb except for clergy. In 1936, he prohibited the veil for women, enforcing Western dress.

Calendar reform: He replaced the Islamic calendar with a Persian imperial one.

Name standardization: Fixed family surnames became mandatory, a practice foreign to Iranian customs.

Women's rights: Women accessed education and some professions, mainly benefiting urban, educated families.

These reforms faced significant resistance, particularly from religious conservatives and rural populations. The forced unveiling of women was especially contentious.

Nationalism and Persian Identity

Reza Shah promoted Persian nationalism as a unifying force, emphasizing Iran's pre-Islamic heritage and downplaying its Islamic identity. This alienated religious conservatives and ethnic minorities. In 1935, the regime changed the country's international name from "Persia" to "Iran," reflecting nationalist ideology.

Western Influence and Resistance

The Paradox of Modernization

Reza Shah's modernization presented a contradiction. While seeking to reduce foreign interference, his reforms were Western-inspired. He hired Western advisors, imported technology, and adopted administrative systems.

This paradox linked modernization with Westernization, perceived as eroding traditional values. Critics argued the shah replaced British and Russian domination with Western cultural imperialism.

Oil and Foreign Interests

Iran's oil complicated efforts to reduce foreign influence. The Anglo-Persian Oil Company controlled production through a 1901 concession favoring British interests.

Reza Shah tried renegotiating the concession in 1932, temporarily canceling it for better terms. Despite some improvements, British control remained substantial, fueling nationalist resentment that contributed to later political upheavals.

Religious Opposition

The Shi'a clergy emerged as primary resistance to reforms threatening clerical authority, income, and influence.

Key opposition sources included:

- Replacement of religious courts with secular systems
- State control over religious endowments
- Forced unveiling of women
- Emphasis on Persian over Islamic identity
- Restriction of religious education

Reza Shah repressed religious opposition through imprisonment, exile, and security force intervention, driving opposition underground.

World War II and Abdication

Reza Shah's efforts crumbled during World War II. Concern over his Nazi sympathies and strategic needs led Britain and the Soviet Union to invade Iran in 1941.

The invasion exposed military weaknesses, leading to his abdication in favor of his son, Mohammad Reza Shah Pahlavi.

Reza Shah died in exile in 1944. His forced abdication underscored the limits of Iranian sovereignty and the persistent power of foreign intervention.

Legacy of Resistance

The Pahlavi modernization left lasting societal tensions. Urban, educated Iranians supported changes, while traditional, religious, and rural populations resisted.

These divisions intensified under Mohammad Reza Shah, contributing to the 1979 revolution. The revolution highlighted that rapid modernization imposed without consensus generated significant opposition.

The Pahlavi era established patterns that shaped Iranian politics: tension between modernization and tradition, conflict between secular and religious authority, and struggles over foreign influence.

Common Misconceptions About the Rise of the Shah

Misconception 1: Reza Shah was simply a Western puppet.

While he adopted Western models, Reza Shah prioritized strengthening Iranian sovereignty and independence, despite methods that paradoxically increased Western influence.

Misconception 2: All Iranians opposed modernization.

Opposition was significant but not universal. Many urban, educated Iranians supported modernization, secularization, and women's rights. Resistance came mainly from religious conservatives and traditional communities.

Misconception 3: The Constitutional Revolution of 1906 established democracy in Iran.

The Revolution created a constitutional monarchy but did not establish a functioning democracy. Political instability and foreign interference hindered genuine representative government.

Misconception 4: Reza Shah's reforms were entirely negative.

Despite controversy and authoritarianism, many reforms in infrastructure, education, and public health offered lasting benefits. However, rapid modernization without consensus led to deep resentments.

Misconception 5: The 1941 Allied invasion was about Reza Shah's Nazi sympathies.

While Reza Shah maintained German relations, the invasion was strategically motivated - securing supply routes and preventing Axis influence was the primary goal.

Quick Summary

Key Takeaways:

- Reza Khan's 1921 coup ended Qājār rule and led to the Pahlavi dynasty's establishment in 1926.

- Reza Shah pursued rapid modernization, including infrastructure, legal reform, secularization, and social transformation.

- While aiming for independence, his program adopted Western models, creating a paradox.

- Religious conservatives, notably the Shi'a clergy, resisted secularization and social reforms.

- The Trans-Iranian Railway symbolized Iranian independence, funded without foreign assistance.

- World War II exposed Iranian sovereignty limits, leading to Reza Shah's abdication.

- Mohammad Reza Shah inherited both the modernization program and its tensions.

- The Pahlavi era laid foundations for lasting divisions between modernist and traditionalist forces, influencing Iranian politics and culminating in the 1979 revolution.

Chapter 15
Oil and Foreign Power

The discovery of oil in Persia fundamentally transformed Iran's relationship with the outside world. What began as a commercial venture in the early 20th century evolved into a geopolitical struggle that would shape Iran's destiny for generations. This chapter examines how the oil beneath Iranian soil became both a blessing and a curse - bringing wealth and modernization while simultaneously making the country a target for foreign manipulation.

The events of the 1950s, particularly the 1953 coup that overthrew a democratically elected government, remain among the most consequential moments in modern Iranian history. Understanding this period is essential for comprehending Iran's subsequent trajectory and its complex relationship with Western powers.

The Discovery of Oil

In the early 1900s, Persia was predominantly agrarian and economically underdeveloped. Few could have predicted that beneath its arid landscapes lay one of the world's most valuable resources.

The story began with British entrepreneur William Knox D'Arcy, who secured a concession from the Persian government in 1901 to explore for oil. D'Arcy hired British geologist George Bernard Reynolds to lead exploration efforts across southwestern Persia.

The work was grueling and expensive. For years, Reynolds and his team drilled through harsh terrain under extreme conditions, finding nothing but dry wells and mounting debts. D'Arcy nearly abandoned the venture.

The Breakthrough at Masjed Soleyman

Success finally came in May 1908 when Reynolds' team struck oil at Masjed Soleyman in southwestern Persia. The discovery was spectacular - a massive gusher that confirmed Persia possessed commercially viable petroleum reserves.

On April 14, 1909, the Burmah Oil Company formed the Anglo-Persian Oil Company (APOC) to exploit these newfound resources. This marked the beginning of industrial-scale oil production in the Middle East.

Transforming the British Navy

The timing proved fortuitous for Britain. Winston Churchill, then First Lord of the Admiralty, was converting the Royal Navy from coal to oil power, seeking faster, more efficient warships. Persian oil offered a secure supply outside British coal mines.

In 1914, the British government purchased a controlling 51% stake in APOC, making it a quasi-governmental entity. This decision intertwined British strategic interests with Persian oil for decades to come.

Early Impact on Persia

Oil revenues began flowing into Persia, though the terms heavily favored APOC. The company built infrastructure, including the massive Abadan refinery complex, one of the world's largest.

However, most profits went to British shareholders rather than the Persian government. This imbalance sowed seeds of resentment that grew throughout the following decades.

Foreign Control and Interests

As oil production expanded, so did foreign influence over Iran's most valuable asset. The relationship between the Iranian government and

APOC (later renamed Anglo-Iranian Oil Company, or AIOC) grew increasingly contentious.

Unequal Terms

The original D'Arcy Concession granted APOC sweeping rights across most of Persia for 60 years. The company controlled exploration, production, and pricing with minimal Iranian oversight.

Iranian officials received only 16% of net profits - a fraction of the wealth extracted from their soil. Meanwhile, AIOC paid more in taxes to the British government than in royalties to Iran.

The Abadan refinery employed thousands of Iranians, but British managers occupied all senior positions. Iranian workers faced discrimination, receiving lower wages and inferior housing compared to British employees.

Growing Iranian Nationalism

By the 1940s, Iranian nationalism was surging. The Constitutional Revolution's legacy had created expectations of sovereignty and self-determination. Many Iranians viewed AIOC as a continuation of British imperialism.

Intellectuals, politicians, and ordinary citizens increasingly questioned why foreigners controlled Iran's most valuable resource. The contrast between British wealth and Iranian poverty in oil-producing regions became impossible to ignore.

Post-World War II Tensions

World War II temporarily occupied Iran, with British and Soviet forces using the country as a supply corridor. This occupation reinforced feelings of vulnerability and foreign manipulation.

After the war, Cold War dynamics added new pressures. The United States and Soviet Union competed for influence across the Middle East. Iran's strategic location and oil reserves made it a prize both superpowers coveted.

The Push for Nationalization

By 1950, calls for nationalizing the oil industry dominated Iranian politics. Nationalization meant transferring ownership and control from AIOC to the Iranian government—a radical but increasingly popular idea.

Mohammed Mossadegh emerged as the leading advocate for nationalization. A European-educated lawyer and seasoned politician, Mossadegh combined nationalist fervor with democratic principles. His speeches electrified crowds and unified diverse political factions behind oil nationalization.

In 1951, the Iranian parliament (Majlis) voted overwhelmingly to nationalize the oil industry. Mossadegh became Prime Minister shortly afterward, tasked with implementing this historic decision.

The British government reacted with fury, viewing nationalization as theft of British property and a dangerous precedent for other oil-producing nations.

The 1953 Coup

The nationalization crisis triggered one of the most controversial episodes in modern Middle Eastern history - a foreign-backed coup that overthrew Iran's democratically elected government.

The Abadan Crisis

Following nationalization, Britain orchestrated an international boycott of Iranian oil. British technicians left the Abadan refinery, and the Royal Navy blockaded Iranian ports to prevent oil exports.

The boycott devastated Iran's economy. Oil revenues plummeted, unemployment soared, and the government struggled to maintain basic services. Britain hoped economic pressure would force Iran to reverse nationalization.

Mossadegh refused to back down. He appealed to international bodies and sought alternative buyers, but British diplomatic pressure proved effective. Few countries dared purchase Iranian oil.

Cold War Calculations

Initially, the United States remained neutral. President Truman's administration sympathized with Iranian nationalism and viewed British colonialism as outdated.

However, when Dwight Eisenhower became president in 1953, American policy shifted. British intelligence convinced Washington that Mossadegh was vulnerable to communist influence, particularly from Iran's Tudeh Party.

The specter of Soviet expansion terrified American policymakers. Losing Iran to communism would threaten Middle Eastern oil supplies and shift the Cold War balance dramatically.

Operation Ajax

In August 1953, the CIA and British Secret Intelligence Service (SIS) executed Operation Ajax—a covert plan to remove Mossadegh from power.

The operation involved:

- Bribing military officers, politicians, and newspaper editors
- Organizing street protests and riots to create chaos
- Spreading propaganda portraying Mossadegh as incompetent or a communist
- Coordinating with royalist military units loyal to the Shah

Initially, the coup attempt failed. The Shah fled to Rome, and Mossadegh appeared to have survived. But within days, a second wave of demonstrations and military action succeeded.

On August 19, 1953, military units arrested Mossadegh. General Fazlollah Zahedi, a pro-Western officer, was installed as Prime Minister. The Shah returned triumphantly from exile.

Immediate Aftermath

Mossadegh was tried for treason and sentenced to house arrest, where he remained until his death in 1967. His supporters faced imprisonment or exile.

The oil industry was reorganized under a consortium that gave American and British companies controlling shares, though Iran received better financial terms than before nationalization.

Long-Term Consequences

Early oil workers in Iran

The 1953 coup's effects rippled through Iranian society and international relations for decades, fundamentally altering Iran's political trajectory.

Strengthened Authoritarianism

The coup consolidated the Shah's power, transforming him from a constitutional monarch into an autocratic ruler. With American backing, he built an extensive security apparatus, including the notorious SAVAK secret police.

Democratic institutions withered. The Majlis became a rubber stamp, opposition parties were suppressed, and political dissent was met with imprisonment or torture. The brief democratic opening of the early 1950s closed permanently.

Anti-Western Resentment

Many Iranians never forgot that foreign powers had overthrown their elected government. The coup became a symbol of Western hypocrisy - promoting democracy abroad while crushing it when inconvenient.

This resentment simmered beneath the surface for 25 years, eventually exploding in the 1979 Islamic Revolution. Revolutionary leaders explicitly cited the 1953 coup as justification for their anti-American stance.

Cold War Alliance

Iran became a key Western ally during the Cold War. The United States provided military aid, training, and diplomatic support. Iran served as a buffer against Soviet expansion and a reliable oil supplier.

However, this alliance came at a cost. The Shah's dependence on American support made him appear as a Western puppet to many Iranians, further eroding his legitimacy.

The Resource Curse in Action

Iran's experience exemplified the "resource curse"—the paradox where countries with abundant natural resources often experience slower economic growth and more authoritarian governance than resource-poor nations.

Oil wealth funded the Shah's military and security forces but didn't translate into broad-based prosperity. Corruption flourished, inequality widened, and economic development remained uneven.

Lasting Distrust

The coup created deep, lasting distrust between Iran and Western powers, particularly the United States and Britain. This distrust continues to shape Iranian foreign policy and complicates diplomatic efforts.

In 1954, the Anglo-Iranian Oil Company rebranded itself as British Petroleum (BP), symbolically distancing itself from the controversy while maintaining substantial Middle Eastern operations.

Common Misconceptions

Misconception 1: The coup was solely about oil profits

While oil was central, Cold War fears of Soviet expansion were equally important. American policymakers genuinely believed Iran might fall to communism, threatening broader Western interests in the Middle East.

Misconception 2: Mossadegh was a communist

Mossadegh was a nationalist and democrat, not a communist. Though he accepted support from Iran's communist Tudeh Party, he remained committed to parliamentary democracy and private property rights.

Misconception 3: The coup was entirely a CIA operation

The coup was a joint CIA-British SIS operation. Britain initiated the planning, and both intelligence services collaborated closely throughout. Iranian royalists and military officers also played crucial roles.

Misconception 4: Iran received no benefits from oil before nationalization

Iran did receive royalties from AIOC, though the terms were highly unfavorable. The issue wasn't zero compensation but the vast disparity between British profits and Iranian returns.

Misconception 5: The 1979 Revolution was inevitable after the coup

While the coup contributed to revolutionary sentiment, the 1979 Revolution resulted from multiple factors accumulated over 25 years, including the Shah's authoritarianism, rapid modernization, and religious opposition.

Key Takeaways:

- George Bernard Reynolds discovered oil in Persia in 1908, leading to the formation of the Anglo-Persian Oil Company in 1909.

- Britain secured a controlling interest in Iranian oil, with terms giving Iran only 16% of net profits.

- Growing Iranian nationalism led to parliament voting to nationalize the oil industry in 1951 under Prime Minister Mohammed Mossadegh.

- The 1953 CIA-British coup overthrew Mossadegh and reinstated the Shah as an authoritarian, pro-Western ruler.

- The coup strengthened Western control over Iranian oil but generated deep resentment that contributed to the 1979 Revolution.

- Iran's experience illustrated the "resource curse"—how oil wealth can paradoxically hinder democratic development.

- The Anglo-Iranian Oil Company became British Petroleum (BP) in 1954, distancing itself from the controversy.

- Cold War fears of Soviet expansion motivated American involvement as much as oil interests.

Chapter 16
The Road to Revolution

The French Revolution remains one of history's most transformative events, reshaping not only France but the entire Western world. Between 1787 and 1799, a nation built on monarchy, aristocratic privilege, and rigid social hierarchy collapsed under its own contradictions. What began with protests over bread prices and tax burdens escalated into a complete overthrow of the established order, culminating in the execution of a king and the birth of radical new ideas about citizenship, equality, and human rights.

This chapter examines the critical period leading to revolution - the mounting pressures that made conflict inevitable. We explore the economic crisis that bankrupted the nation, the social divisions that fueled explosive resentment, the religious tensions that undermined traditional authority, and the cascade of protests that ultimately toppled the monarchy.

Understanding this road to revolution reveals how long-standing problems, poor leadership, and popular anger can combine to produce dramatic historical change. The lessons of 1789 remain relevant today, offering insights into how societies fracture and transform under pressure.

Social and Economic Tensions

France in the 1780s faced a deepening financial catastrophe. Decades of deficit spending, costly wars, and extravagant royal expenditure had pushed the nation to the brink of bankruptcy. Involvement in the American Revolution, while politically satisfying for France's rivalry with Britain, proved financially devastating. The national debt spiraled out of control, and the government struggled to meet basic obligations.

The Three Estates System

French society operated under a rigid hierarchy divided into three estates. The First Estate consisted of the clergy, the Second Estate comprised the nobility, and the Third Estate included everyone else - from wealthy merchants to impoverished peasants. This system created profound inequality.

The Third Estate, representing roughly 98% of the population, bore nearly the entire tax burden.

Meanwhile, the clergy and nobility enjoyed extensive exemptions and privileges. Peasants paid feudal dues, church tithes, royal taxes, and other fees, often consuming half or more of their income.

Economic Crisis Deepens

Charles-Alexandre de Calonne, Controller-General of Finances, attempted reforms to address the crisis by proposing to tax the previously exempt nobility and clergy. These efforts met fierce resistance, as the aristocracy refused to surrender their advantages, blocking meaningful reform.

Simultaneously, poor harvests in the late 1780s drove food prices upward. Bread, the staple of the French diet, became increasingly unaffordable. Urban workers spent up to 80% of their wages on bread alone during the worst periods. Rural peasants faced similar hardships.

Growing Resentment

The contrast between the suffering of common people and the opulence of Versailles fueled mounting anger. While peasants starved, the royal court maintained its lavish lifestyle. King Louis XVI's administration proved unable to address these fundamental problems effectively.

As the Third Estate's discontent grew, educated middle-class members - lawyers, doctors, merchants - recognized the injustice of their exclusion from political power despite their economic contributions. This combination of financial crisis, social inequality, and political rigidity created a powder keg awaiting ignition.

Religious Opposition

The Catholic Church occupied a unique position in pre-revolutionary France as the First Estate, wielding considerable wealth and influence. However, the relationship between church, state, and society grew increasingly strained as Enlightenment ideas challenged traditional religious authority.

Church Wealth and Privilege

The Church owned about 10% of French land and collected mandatory tithes from all citizens. While church officials enjoyed tax exemptions, ordinary clergy often lived in poverty. This disparity created tensions within the church itself, as lower-ranking priests sympathized with common people's struggles.

The church's close alliance with the monarchy made it a target for those opposing the existing order. Critics viewed the institution as complicit in maintaining an unjust system that perpetuated inequality and suffering.

Enlightenment Challenges

Enlightenment philosophers had questioned religious dogma and promoted reason, science, and individual rights. Voltaire's attacks on church corruption and Rousseau's ideas about popular sovereignty undermined traditional religious authority.

These ideas spread through salons, coffeehouses, and pamphlets, reaching educated members of the Third Estate. Many began viewing the church as an obstacle to progress rather than a moral guide.

Clergy Divisions

Many lower-ranking priests, living modestly and working directly with poor communities, recognized the system's injustices. When the

Estates-General convened in 1789, some clergy sided with the Third Estate rather than their traditional allies.

This split within the church weakened its ability to defend the old order. Progressive clergy provided moral legitimacy to revolutionary demands, arguing that true Christian principles supported equality and justice.

Revolutionary Reforms

As the revolution progressed, the National Constituent Assembly implemented sweeping reforms. The Civil Constitution of the Clergy subordinated the church to state authority, requiring clergy to swear loyalty oaths to the nation rather than the Pope.

These measures alienated conservative Catholics while satisfying those who saw the church as an impediment to reform. Religious opposition thus became both a cause and consequence of revolutionary upheaval, with the church's traditional role permanently altered.

Protests and Unrest

The transition from discontent to open rebellion occurred through escalating protests and confrontations. Economic hardship, political frustration, and new ideas about rights and representation combined to produce unprecedented popular mobilization.

The Estates-General Convenes

Facing financial collapse, Louis XVI convened the Estates-General in May 1789 - the first meeting since 1614. Each estate traditionally voted as a bloc, allowing the First and Second Estates to outvote the Third Estate despite representing a tiny fraction of the population.

The Third Estate demanded vote-by-head rather than vote-by-estate, which would give them fair representation. When this request was denied, representatives declared themselves the National Assembly in June 1789, vowing to remain until France had a constitution.

The Tennis Court Oath

Locked out of their meeting hall, National Assembly members gathered at a nearby tennis court on June 20, 1789, swearing the Tennis Court Oath - a pledge to remain together until their goals were achieved. This act marked a decisive break with royal authority.

Louis XVI initially resisted but eventually ordered the First and Second Estates to join the National Assembly, while concentrating troops around Paris, suggesting force might be used to dissolve the assembly.

Storming of the Bastille

Rumors of military action sparked panic. On July 14, 1789, crowds stormed the Bastille, a royal fortress symbolizing monarchical tyranny. Its fall represented the people's power to challenge royal authority directly.

The event electrified France. Bastille Day became a revolutionary symbol, demonstrating that ordinary citizens could successfully resist the king's forces. Louis XVI reportedly asked an advisor, "Is it a revolt?" The advisor responded, "No, sire, it is a revolution."

Rural Uprisings

Unrest spread beyond Paris. In the countryside, peasants attacked noble estates, burning feudal records documenting their obligations. This "Great Fear" swept through rural France during summer 1789.

The National Assembly responded by abolishing the feudal system in August 1789, eliminating noble privileges and feudal dues - a reform that fundamentally restructured French society.

Women's March on Versailles

In October 1789, thousands of Parisian women marched to Versailles demanding bread and political reform. They forced the royal family to return to Paris, showing that revolutionary energy came from all segments of society.

The Collapse of the Monarchy

The monarchy's authority eroded steadily between 1789 and 1792, culminating in its complete abolition. Louis XVI's inability to adapt to revolutionary change, combined with foreign threats and radical political developments, sealed the institution's fate.

Constitutional Monarchy Fails

Initially, revolutionaries sought to transform rather than eliminate the monarchy. The Constitution of 1791 established a constitutional monarchy with Louis XVI as head of state but with severely limited powers.

Louis XVI appeared to accept this arrangement, but his commitment remained questionable. In June 1791, the royal family attempted to flee France, hoping to reach Austria. Guards captured them at Varennes and they returned to Paris in humiliation.

This flight attempt destroyed remaining trust in the king. Many concluded that Louis XVI opposed the revolution and would betray it given the opportunity. Radical factions gained influence, arguing that monarchy itself was incompatible with liberty.

War and Radicalization

In April 1792, France declared war on Austria, beginning the French Revolutionary Wars. European monarchies viewed the revolution with alarm, fearing similar uprisings. France faced a coalition of hostile powers determined to restore the old order.

Military setbacks and invasion threats intensified revolutionary fervor. Radicals accused moderates of insufficient commitment, while suspicion of counter-revolutionary conspiracies grew. The political atmosphere became increasingly volatile.

Abolition of Monarchy

On August 10, 1792, Parisian crowds stormed the Tuileries Palace, overwhelming the king's Swiss Guards. The National Assembly suspended the monarchy, calling for elections to a new National Convention. In September 1792, this Convention formally abolished the monarchy and established the First French Republic.

Louis XVI faced trial for treason in December 1792. The Convention debated his fate, with some arguing for exile and others demanding execution. On January 21, 1793, Louis XVI was guillotined in Paris's Place de la Révolution. His execution symbolized the complete break with France's monarchical past.

The Reign of Terror

Revolutionary government grew increasingly radical under pressure from war and internal opposition. Maximilien Robespierre emerged as a dominant figure, advocating ruthless measures against perceived enemies of the revolution. The Committee of Public Safety initiated the Reign of Terror.

Between 1793 and 1794, revolutionary tribunals executed thousands of suspected counter-revolutionaries, including Queen Marie Antoinette and former revolutionary leaders. The guillotine became the revolution's symbol.

The Terror ended with Robespierre's own execution in July 1794 during the Thermidorian Reaction, demonstrating the revolution's tendency to consume its own leaders. Political instability continued until Napoleon Bonaparte seized power in 1799.

Legacy of Collapse

The monarchy's collapse transformed European politics. Revolutionary France demonstrated that royal authority was not permanent. Ideas about popular sovereignty, citizenship, and equality spread across Europe, inspiring future movements and revolutions.

Napoleon's rise and conquests carried revolutionary principles throughout Europe, even as he established his own imperial rule. The tension between revolutionary ideals and authoritarian practice would characterize French politics for decades.

Common Misconceptions About the French Revolution

Misconception: The Revolution was primarily about overthrowing a tyrannical king.

Reality: While Louis XVI's ineffectiveness contributed to the crisis, the revolution stemmed from systemic issues - financial collapse, social inequality, and political rigidity.

Misconception: The Bastille held hundreds of political prisoners when it was stormed.

Reality: The Bastille had only seven prisoners on July 14, 1789. Its symbolic importance as a representation of royal authority far exceeded its practical significance.

Misconception: The Revolution immediately established democracy and equality.

Reality: The revolutionary period saw competing visions and conflicts. True democracy remained limited, and many revolutionary ideals took generations to implement.

Misconception: The Reign of Terror was necessary to save the revolution.

Reality: Historians debate whether the Terror's measures were justified or represented an excess that undermined revolutionary principles.

Misconception: Napoleon betrayed the revolution by becoming emperor.

Reality: Napoleon preserved some revolutionary achievements while abandoning others. His relationship to revolutionary ideals remains complex.

Quick Summary

Key Takeaways:

- **Financial crisis and social inequality** created explosive tensions in 1780s France, with the Third Estate bearing crushing tax burdens while nobility and clergy enjoyed exemptions

- **Religious opposition** emerged as Enlightenment ideas challenged church authority, though clergy themselves divided over supporting or resisting change

- **Popular protests escalated** from the Tennis Court Oath through the Storming of the Bastille to rural uprisings, demonstrating widespread rejection of the old order

- **Constitutional monarchy failed** when Louis XVI's flight attempt destroyed trust, leading to the monarchy's abolition in September 1792

- **Louis XVI's execution** in January 1793 symbolized the complete break with monarchical tradition and France's commitment to republican government

- **The Reign of Terror** (1793-1794) represented revolutionary radicalism, with Robespierre leading mass executions before his own downfall

- **Revolutionary impact extended beyond France**, spreading ideas about popular sovereignty that influenced European politics for generations

- **Napoleon's rise** emerged from revolutionary chaos, preserving some achievements while establishing new forms of authoritarian rule

Chapter 17
The Islamic Revolution

The Iranian Revolution of 1979 stands as one of the most significant political upheavals of the twentieth century. Within months, millions of Iranians united to overthrow a monarchy that had ruled for decades, replacing it with an Islamic republic under religious leadership. This transformation reshaped not only Iran but also the broader Middle East, introducing a new model of governance that blended religious authority with modern state structures.

This chapter examines the key events of 1979, the rise of Ayatollah Ruhollah Khomeini as the revolution's spiritual and political leader, and the establishment of the Islamic Republic that followed. Understanding this revolution requires recognizing both its immediate triggers - widespread dissatisfaction with Shah Mohammad Reza Pahlavi's autocratic rule - and deeper roots in Iranian society's desire for self-determination and religious identity.

The revolution demonstrated the power of mass nonviolent protest, even against a well-armed regime. It also revealed how religious leadership could mobilize diverse social groups around shared grievances and aspirations. The consequences of these events continue to influence regional politics, international relations, and debates about religion's role in governance.

Key Events of 1979

The climax of the Iranian Revolution occurred in early 1979, after years of accumulating unrest. Between 1977 and 1979, Iran witnessed growing protests and demonstrations that gradually undermined the Shah's authority.

The Escalation of Protests

By fall 1978, opposition to the Shah's regime reached its zenith. Millions of Iranians took to the streets in some of the largest public protests in modern history. These demonstrations included peaceful marches, business boycotts, and mass sit-ins that paralyzed major cities.

The protest movement's diversity was its strength, with participants from across Iranian society: students, workers, merchants, religious scholars, and middle-class professionals. This broad representation ensured the movement could not be dismissed as the voice of a single group.

Nonviolent Resistance

Despite violent repression from the Shah's security forces, the protests remained largely nonviolent. Tactics included general strikes that shut down oil production and commerce, peaceful marches that filled city streets, and collective prayer gatherings that doubled as political demonstrations.

Each act of repression by the Shah's forces intensified opposition, creating an unsustainable situation for the monarchy.

The Shah's Abdication

As protests escalated and the economy stalled, the Shah's position became untenable. Traditional supporters, including business leaders and some military officers, began to withdraw their backing.

In January 1979, the Shah left Iran, ostensibly for medical treatment, effectively abdicating his throne. His departure marked the end of the Pahlavi dynasty and cleared the way for revolutionary forces to take power.

February 11, 1979: The Monarchy Falls

On February 11, 1979, revolutionary forces took control of government buildings, military installations, and state media, marking the formal collapse of the monarchy. The speed of this collapse astonished observers, as a seemingly entrenched regime crumbled once the Shah was gone.

The Rise of Khomeini

Ruhollah Khomeini emerged as the undisputed leader of the Iranian Revolution, evolving from an exiled religious scholar to the architect of a new Islamic state. His rise reflected his personal authority and ability to articulate a vision that resonated with millions.

Background and Exile

Khomeini, a senior Shi'i religious scholar, had long opposed the Shah's secular modernization and authoritarian policies. His criticisms in the 1960s led to his arrest and eventual exile in 1964.

From exile - first in Iraq, then France - Khomeini maintained influence through recorded speeches and messages smuggled into Iran. These communications reached a wide audience, establishing him as a dominant voice of opposition.

Ideological Leadership

Khomeini's vision involved establishing an Islamic government guided by religious principles and led by qualified scholars. He posited that true justice and independence required Islamic governance, free from Western influence and the Shah's corruption.

His message resonated widely, combining religious authority with populist themes against economic inequality, political repression, and foreign interference.

Unifying Symbol

Shi'i Islam served as a unifying cultural and religious element. Khomeini skillfully used religious symbolism and networks to mobilize support, with mosques becoming centers of organization and religious occasions serving as covers for political gatherings.

This religious dimension set the Iranian Revolution apart from other twentieth-century revolutions, with its identity deeply shaped by Islamic principles.

Return to Iran

In February 1979, Khomeini returned to Iran after fifteen years of exile, greeted by millions lining the streets of Tehran. This reception underscored his status as the revolution's leader.

Khomeini quickly began consolidating power and shaping the post-revolutionary government, his authority deriving from his religious credentials and leadership.

The Role of the United States

Initially, President Jimmy Carter's administration supported the Shah but shifted as the revolution gained momentum. By late 1978, U.S. officials acknowledged that decisions about Iran's leadership should be determined by Iranians, effectively withdrawing full support.

The Establishment of a New Regime

Following the monarchy's collapse, Iran transformed rapidly as revolutionary forces established new governmental structures under religious leadership.

The Revolutionary Council

Immediately after the Shah's departure, Khomeini and the Revolutionary Council organized a new government, involving religious scholars, political activists, and technocrats opposed to the Shah.

The provisional government included both religious and secular figures, though tensions soon arose over the state's direction.

Transfer of Authority

Within months, the provisional government resigned, transferring full authority to Khomeini and religious institutions. This marked the decisive victory for those advocating an Islamic Republic over secular democratic visions.

The transition included establishing new institutions based on Islamic principles, including religious courts, revolutionary committees, and the position of Supreme Leader - occupied by Khomeini.

The Islamic Republic

A March 1979 referendum overwhelmingly approved the establishment of an Islamic Republic. A new constitution enshrined the principle of velayat-e faqih (guardianship of the jurist), granting ultimate authority to qualified religious scholars.

This system created a unique governmental structure, melding elected institutions with religious oversight. The Supreme Leader, appointed by scholars, controlled the military, judiciary, and key policies.

Social Transformation

The new regime implemented sweeping societal changes, with Islamic law as the basis for legal codes. Women faced new dress codes, and Western cultural influences were restricted.

These changes aimed to create a society organized around Islamic principles, distinct from Western models and the Shah's secular modernization.

Regional Impact

The establishment of the Islamic Republic had profound consequences beyond Iran. It inspired Islamic movements globally and challenged existing political orders. The revolution showed that religious leadership could successfully mobilize mass movements and govern modern states.

The new regime's anti-Western stance and support for revolutionary movements continue to shape Middle Eastern politics.

Common Misconceptions About the Iranian Revolution

Misconception: The revolution was solely a religious movement.

Reality: While religious leadership was central, diverse groups supported the revolution, driven by economic, political, and foreign influence grievances. Students, workers, merchants, and intellectuals participated alongside religious activists.

Misconception: The revolution was violent from the start.

Reality: The movement was largely nonviolent, using strikes, boycotts, and peaceful demonstrations. Violence primarily came from the Shah's forces. The revolution's success owed much to sustained nonviolent resistance.

Misconception: Khomeini controlled the revolution from the beginning.

Reality: While Khomeini became the dominant figure, the revolution initially included diverse opposition groups with different visions. His faction consolidated power after the Shah's fall, but this was not predetermined.

Misconception: The United States strongly supported the Shah until the end.

Reality: Although the U.S. initially backed the Shah, the Carter administration grew uncertain as the revolution progressed. By late 1978, U.S. officials acknowledged decisions should be made by Iranians, effectively withdrawing full support.

Misconception: The Islamic Republic's structure was planned in advance.

Reality: The specific governmental structure emerged through post-revolution negotiations and power struggles. The constitution, establishing the Supreme Leader's role, was drafted and approved months after the monarchy fell.

Quick Summary

Key Takeaways:

- The Iranian Revolution of 1979 overthrew the Pahlavi monarchy and established an Islamic Republic under religious leadership.

- Protests between 1977-1979 involved millions of Iranians from diverse backgrounds, united by opposition to the Shah's autocratic rule.

- The revolution was largely nonviolent, employing strikes, boycotts, and peaceful demonstrations despite violent government repression.

- Ayatollah Ruhollah Khomeini emerged as the revolution's leader, using religious authority and populist appeals to mobilize support.

- On February 11, 1979, the monarchy officially fell, marking the beginning of Iran's transformation into an Islamic state.

- The new regime established unique governmental structures combining elected institutions with religious oversight under a Supreme Leader.

- Shi'i Islam served as a unifying force, with mosques and religious networks playing crucial roles.

- The revolution's success reshaped Middle Eastern politics and demonstrated religion's potential as a basis for modern governance.

PART 6
IRAN TODAY

Chapter 18
The Islamic Republic Explained Simply

The 1979 Iranian Revolution not only toppled a monarchy but also established a novel form of governance. The Islamic Republic of Iran merges religious authority with modern political institutions, creating a unique system. Understanding this is key to comprehending modern Iran.

This chapter outlines Iran's governmental structure, the impact of religion on politics, and the centers of real power. We simplify complex institutions to illuminate how Iran's system functions and why it diverges from both traditional monarchies and Western democracies.

The Islamic Republic is not merely a religious state or a typical republic - it is a hybrid where religious leaders exert ultimate authority over elected officials. This dual power structure may initially appear confusing but operates with its own internal logic.

The Structure of Government

The Constitutional Foundation

Iran's Constitution, adopted in 1979 and amended in 1989, serves as its supreme law, establishing a theocratic government markedly different from the monarchy it replaced. The Constitution crafts a complex system with numerous branches, prioritizing religious authority above all institutions.

The Supreme Leader

At Iran's pinnacle of power is the Supreme Leader, appointed for life by the Assembly of Experts, a council of senior religious scholars. The Supreme Leader oversees policies and holds authority over the military, judiciary, and media. This role, unelected by popular vote, represents a significant shift from typical republican governance.

The Guardian Council

The Guardian Council, a powerful oversight body, consists of:

- Six Islamic jurists appointed by the Supreme Leader

- Six legal scholars nominated by the judiciary and approved by Parliament

The council exercises significant power in legislative oversight and electoral supervision, requiring all laws to receive its approval and vetting all candidates for office.

The Elected Government

Iran's dual system comprises both religious and republican elements:

Parliament (Majlis): Elected by popular vote, Parliament legislates on domestic matters, but all laws require Guardian Council approval for compliance with Islamic law.

The President: Also elected, the President leads the executive branch and manages daily government operations but remains subordinate to the Supreme Leader.

Iran's legal system blends Islamic law with elements of French civil law, creating a hybrid framework where all regulations must adhere to Islamic principles.

The Role of Religion in Politics

Theocratic Governance

The Islamic Republic institutionalizes theocracy - making religious law the foundation of political authority. The Constitution mandates governance within an Islamic framework, embedding religious principles into the core of political decision-making.

Velayat-e Faqih (Guardianship of the Jurist)

The system rests on *velayat-e faqih*, the guardianship of the Islamic jurist, asserting that, in the absence of the hidden Imam, religious scholars must guide society. This theological concept justifies religious authority over elected bodies.

Islamic Law in Practice

Sharia law influences all facets of governance:

- **Legislation**: Laws must align with Islamic principles.

- **Judiciary**: Courts apply Islamic jurisprudence.

- **Social policy**: Religious rules are enforced by the state.

- **Economic policy**: Islamic banking eschews interest, requiring alternative financial systems.

Constitutional Goals

The Constitution sets religious objectives, such as promoting Islamic values and ensuring freedoms within Islamic boundaries. These are mandates guiding policy-making.

Balancing Religion and Governance

The system attempts a balance wherein religious principles are paramount, but elected officials handle practical needs like economic development and healthcare. Tensions arise when practical needs clash with religious mandates, with religious authorities maintaining ultimate decision-making power.

Power and Decision-Making

The Concentration of Authority

In Iran's system, real power rests in unelected religious institutions:

Supreme Leader: Commands military, judiciary appointments, media oversight, policy direction, and war declarations.

Guardian Council: Controls legislative approval, candidate eligibility, and constitutional interpretation.

Elected Officials: Handle daily operations within religiously sanctioned boundaries.

The Legislative Process

The legislative process vividly illustrates the interplay between religious and elected authorities, with the Guardian Council wielding veto power.

Electoral Control

The Council's vetting process restricts political participation by disqualifying insufficiently religious or loyal candidates, thus limiting genuine competition.

Military and Security Authority

The Supreme Leader controls military and security bodies, independent from the elected President, providing direct enforcement authority.

Economic Decision-Making

Both religious and elected authorities share roles in economic policy, with the Guardian Council ensuring compliance with Islamic principles and the Supreme Leader holding ultimate decision-making power.

Checks and Balances

Iran's system has internal checks, such as the potential removal of the Supreme Leader by the Assembly of Experts, but religious dominance limits true oversight.

Practical Governance

Elected officials navigate practical governance within religiously defined boundaries, leading to occasional conflicts resolved in favor of religious authority.

Common Misconceptions About Iran's Government

Misconception: Iran is a standard dictatorship.

Reality: It's a complex system with multiple power centers and religious oversight.

Misconception: Iranian elections are meaningless.

Reality: Elections influence policy and direction, despite candidate screening.

Misconception: Iran lacks a modern legal framework.

Reality: It combines Islamic law with modern civil law.

Misconception: The President runs the government.

Reality: The President manages operations but is subordinate to the Supreme Leader.

Misconception: Iran's system mirrors other Islamic countries.

Reality: Iran's theocratic republic is unique, granting political control to religious authorities.

Quick Summary

Key Takeaways:

- Iran's 1979 Constitution established a theocratic republic blending religious and elected institutions.

- The Supreme Leader holds supreme authority over various domains.

- The Guardian Council's approval is requisite for candidates and legislation.

- Elected bodies operate within religious boundaries set by theocratic structures.

- Iran's legal system is a hybrid of Islamic and civil law elements.

- Power resides primarily in unelected religious institutions.

- The system emphasizes self-sufficiency within an Islamic framework.

- Decision-making balances religious parameters with practical governance.

Chapter 19
War and Survival

War transforms nations in profound and lasting ways. For Iran, the eight-year conflict with Iraq, from 1980 to 1988, stands as a devastating chapter in its modern history. This war tested the Iranian people's resilience, reshaped the economy, and left scars that would take decades to heal.

To understand this conflict, it is essential to explore not just the military campaigns but also the profound human and economic toll it exacted on ordinary Iranians. This chapter delves into how Iran endured one of the 20th century's most brutal conflicts, the staggering costs it imposed, and the long road to recovery.

The Iran-Iraq War

Origins and Duration

The Iran-Iraq War began in September 1980 when Iraqi forces invaded Iran, initiating an eight-year conflict. It emerged as one of the longest conventional military engagements of the 20th century and ranks among the bloodiest in Middle Eastern history.

The timing was particularly devastating for Iran, still reeling from the 1979 revolution and subsequent political upheaval. The Iraqi invasion exploited this period of vulnerability, striking when Iran was internally transitioning.

The Nature of the Conflict

The war quickly devolved into a brutal attrition struggle. Both nations committed vast resources, with battles marked by trench warfare reminiscent of World War I. Despite years of fighting, neither side could achieve a decisive victory.

The conflict impacted every facet of Iranian society. Cities endured bombardment, infrastructure crumbled, and the economy redirected entirely to support the war effort. Basic goods became scarce as resources were funneled to the front lines.

Economic Disruption

The war's economic impact was immediate and intensified over time. Prices for basic goods soared as supply chains faltered and production facilities suffered damage. Ordinary Iranians faced shortages of food, medicine, and essential supplies.

Iran's oil industry, the economic backbone, was particularly affected. Oil facilities became frequent targets, significantly reducing production. This loss of revenue compounded the economic crisis, hampering the government's ability to maintain civilian services while financing the war.

Impact on Daily Life

For average Iranians, the war brought profound changes. Families endured rationing, blackouts, and the constant threat of air raids. Many young men were mobilized for military service, stripping communities of their workforce.

Financial pressures were staggering. Economic analyses suggest the average Iranian lost about $34,660 in potential income from 1978 to 1988. This figure reflects not just direct war costs but also lost economic opportunities and reduced quality of life.

The Human Dimension

Beyond statistics, the war's human cost was immense. There was significant loss of life on both sides, with Iranian families across the country mourning casualties. The conflict created widows, orphans, and disabled veterans requiring long-term support.

Public suffering extended beyond combatants. Civilians faced city bombardments, displacement, and the psychological trauma of living under perpetual threat. The war generation of Iranians grew up with air raid sirens and rationing shaping their lives.

International Dimensions

The Iran-Iraq War garnered international attention and involvement, though major powers largely remained neutral or alternated support to both sides. The conflict's protracted nature and intensity marked it as a defining event for the broader Middle East.

The war's persistence showcased both nations' determination and the international community's inability or unwillingness to negotiate peace. Ceasefire talks repeatedly faltered until 1988 when an exhausted Iran and Iraq agreed to a UN-brokered ceasefire.

Human and Economic Costs

Reconstruction Requirements

When the war ended in 1988, Iran faced an enormous rebuilding challenge. Reconstruction costs were estimated at $230 billion, representing widespread destruction of infrastructure, industry, and public facilities.

This sum included damaged oil facilities, destroyed transport networks, and ruined cities. The reconstruction needs spanned every sector, from agriculture to manufacturing to public services.

Long-Term Economic Implications

The war's economic consequences reached far beyond immediate reconstruction. Iran's development trajectory was fundamentally altered, with years of potential growth lost to military expenditure and war damage.

Infrastructure required complete rebuilding. Roads, bridges, and essential systems needed repair or replacement. Industrial facilities needed substantial investment to restore production capacity.

Human Casualties and Social Impact

The human cost was incalculable in economic terms. Casualties created a generation of war-affected families requiring ongoing support. Veterans needed medical care and rehabilitation services for decades.

Community social fabric bore lasting scars. The loss of young men in their prime impacted demographics and economic capacity. Families coped with absent breadwinners, and communities worked to reintegrate veterans into civilian life.

Recovery and Reconstruction

Destroyed city landscape during the Iran–Iraq War

Immediate Post-War Challenges

Iran's recovery began in 1988 under challenging conditions. The government faced demobilizing military forces while rebuilding critical infrastructure. Resources remained scarce, and the economy required restructuring to transition from wartime to peacetime production.

Priority areas included restoring oil production, rebuilding cities, and reestablishing essential services. Balancing immediate humanitarian needs with long-term planning was crucial.

Economic Restructuring

Recovery demanded more than rebuilding. Iran needed to modernize its economy and reduce oil dependency. This slow, challenging process was complicated by international sanctions and limited foreign investment.

Reconstruction required enormous financial resources when the treasury was depleted. Iran prioritized projects vital to broader economic recovery.

Long-Term Recovery Process

Recovery extended far beyond immediate post-war years. Decades later, Iran continued addressing war-related challenges. Reconstructing $230 billion in damages necessitated sustained effort and investment.

Recovery involved not only physical rebuilding but also social and economic healing. Iran worked to reintegrate veterans, support affected families, and rebuild devastated communities, shaping society and policy long after the conflict ended.

Common Misconceptions About the Iran-Iraq War

Misconception 1: The war was primarily about religious differences

While religion featured in propaganda, political, territorial, and economic motives, including border disputes, were key factors.

Misconception 2: The war ended with a clear victor

Neither country achieved its war goals. The 1988 ceasefire restored pre-war borders, resulting in a costly stalemate.

Misconception 3: Iran quickly recovered after 1988

Recovery took decades. The $230 billion reconstruction cost and loss of human capital presented long-term challenges.

Misconception 4: The economic impact only affected the war years

The average Iranian's $34,660 lost income during 1978-1988 represents just the immediate impact. Long-term consequences persisted.

Misconception 5: The war's impact was primarily military

The conflict reshaped Iran's society, economy, and demographics, affecting all aspects of civilian life.

Key Takeaways:

- The Iran-Iraq War (1980-1988) ranks among the 20th century's bloodiest conflicts.

- Reconstruction costs were estimated at $230 billion, reflecting massive damage.

- Average Iranians lost approximately $34,660 in potential income from 1978 to 1988.

- The conflict caused significant loss of life and created lasting social challenges.

- Recovery and reconstruction took decades and fundamentally altered Iran's trajectory.

- The war ended in a costly stalemate, with no decisive victory.

Chapter 20
Iran vs The World

For over seventy years, Iran's interactions with the global community - especially the United States - have been characterized by cycles of cooperation, confrontation, and crisis. From Cold War alliances to revolutionary upheaval, diplomatic breakthroughs to military strikes, Iran's position on the world stage reflects deep historical wounds, competing national interests, and the persistent challenge of nuclear ambitions.

This chapter explores three critical facets of Iran's global relationships: its complex and often hostile relationship with the United States, economic warfare through international sanctions, and the nuclear program that has dominated diplomacy for decades. Understanding these interconnected issues reveals not only Iran's strategic calculations but also broader geopolitical forces shaping Middle Eastern politics and global security.

Relations with the United States

The Foundation of Mistrust

U.S.-Iran hostility originates in August 1953 when American and British intelligence agencies orchestrated a coup against Iran's democratically elected Prime Minister Mohammad Mossadeq. Mossadeq had nationalized Iran's oil industry, threatening Western petroleum interests. The coup reinstated Shah Mohammad Reza Pahlavi, establishing a pro-Western authoritarian regime that lasted 26 years.

This intervention sowed seeds of resentment that shaped Iranian politics for generations. Many Iranians viewed the Shah as an American puppet, and his increasingly repressive rule - supported by

U.S. military and intelligence - became synonymous with foreign interference.

Revolution and Rupture

The 1979 Iranian Revolution transformed U.S.-Iran relations. Ayatollah Ruhollah Khomeini's overthrow of the Shah established an Islamic Republic explicitly opposed to American influence. The revolution's anti-Western ideology made confrontation with the United States a defining feature of the new regime.

The breaking point came on November 4, 1979, when Iranian students stormed the U.S. Embassy in Tehran, taking 52 Americans hostage. The crisis lasted 444 days, humiliating the United States on the world stage. For Americans, the hostage crisis symbolized Iranian radicalism. For Iranians, it was a final rejection of decades of U.S. interference.

The hostage crisis severed diplomatic relations between the countries - a rupture that remains.

Decades of Hostility

Throughout the 1980s and 1990s, hostility persisted. The U.S. supported Iraq during the Iran-Iraq War (1980-1988), providing intelligence and military assistance to Saddam Hussein. Iran supported militant groups like Hezbollah, earning its designation as a state sponsor of terrorism.

Despite occasional diplomatic overtures, mistrust prevailed, each side viewing the other through past grievances: Americans recalled the hostage crisis, while Iranians remembered the 1953 coup.

The Modern Era: Diplomacy and Confrontation

The early 21st century saw both diplomatic progress and renewed conflict. Between 2013 and 2015, the Obama adminstration engaged in negotiations over Iran's nuclear program, leading to the Joint Comprehensive Plan of Action (JCPOA), the most significant diplomatic breakthrough since 1979.

However, in 2018, President Donald Trump withdrew the United States from the nuclear deal, reinstituting maximum pressure policies and economic sanctions.

Tensions peaked in January 2020 when a U.S. drone strike in Baghdad assassinated General Qassem Soleimani, Iran's elite Quds Force commander. Iran retaliated with missile strikes against U.S. bases in Iraq.

Confrontation continued into the mid-2020s, with U.S. air strikes on Iranian nuclear facilities in June 2025, leading to broader military operations in 2026 - marking the most direct military engagement between the nations in modern history.

Sanctions and Economic Pressure

The Strategy of Economic Warfare

Economic sanctions have been a primary tool Western powers - led by the United States - used to pressure Iran. Rather than invade militarily, sanctions aim to inflict severe economic pain to force policy changes, particularly regarding Iran's nuclear program and regional activities.

By restricting Iran's access to international markets, banking systems, and technologies, the international community seeks to limit the regime's resources and create domestic pressure for compromise.

Layers of Sanctions

Iran faces multiple layers of sanctions from different entities:

U.S. Unilateral Sanctions: These target Iran's energy sector, financial institutions, and military industries. American sanctions also include secondary sanctions on foreign companies doing business with Iran, forcing international firms to choose between Iranian and U.S. markets.

United Nations Sanctions: Between 2006 and 2015, the UN Security Council imposed sanctions related to Iran's nuclear program, including arms embargoes and travel bans.

European Union Sanctions: Coordinated with broader international efforts, EU sanctions target the oil sector and financial transactions to pressure Iran on nuclear issues.

Economic Impact

Sanctions have devastated Iran's economy:

- **Oil Revenue Collapse**: Sanctions have drastically reduced Iranian oil exports, a primary foreign currency source.

- **Currency Devaluation**: Inflation has spiked, reducing purchasing power for ordinary Iranians.

- **Banking Isolation**: Exclusion from international banking systems has complicated Iran's international trade.

- **Technology Restrictions**: Sanctions hinder modernization of critical sectors like oil infrastructure and aviation.

The Nuclear Deal and Sanctions Relief

The 2015 nuclear agreement offered Iran sanctions relief in exchange for limits on its nuclear program. For a time, Iran regained access to international markets, and European companies reengaged.

However, President Trump's 2018 withdrawal and re-imposition of sanctions led to the end of Iran's brief economic recovery.

Humanitarian Consequences and Debate

Sanctions have ignited debates about effectiveness and humanitarian impact. Critics argue sanctions harm ordinary Iranians, limiting access to medicine and opportunities, without fundamentally changing regime behavior.

Supporters see sanctions as necessary alternatives to military action.

Sanctions have damaged Iran's economy and constrained capabilities, but the desired policy shifts remain elusive, leaving sanctions a persistent aspect of Iran's international isolation.

The Nuclear Issue

Origins of Iran's Nuclear Program

Iran's nuclear program began in the 1950s with U.S. support. Under the Shah, Iran pursued nuclear energy as part of modernization. The 1979 revolution paused these efforts, but Iran resumed nuclear activities in the 1980s.

Concerns mounted in the early 2000s when evidence suggested Iran was developing uranium enrichment capabilities.

The International Crisis

The dual-use nature of enrichment technology sparked international alarm. While Iran claimed its program was for peaceful purposes, Western powers feared potential nuclear weapons development.

Key concerns included underground enrichment facilities, weapons research allegations, and potential regional arms race implications.

Diplomatic Efforts

International diplomacy focused on constraining Iran's nuclear program. The UN passed resolutions demanding Iran suspend enrichment activities, leading to severe sanctions when Iran refused.

Intermittent negotiations between Iran and world powers made little progress until 2013.

The 2015 Nuclear Deal

Under President Obama, secret negotiations led to the JCPOA in 2015, representing a compromise:

Iran agreed to:

- Reduce its enriched uranium stockpile by 98%
- Limit enrichment to civilian-use levels
- Allow international inspectors access
- Accept restrictions on nuclear research

In exchange, Iran received:

- Sanctions relief
- Access to frozen assets
- Renewed ability to sell oil internationally

The deal extended the "breakout time" for weapons-grade uranium to at least a year.

Collapse of the Agreement

The nuclear deal faced criticism, with opponents arguing it was insufficient. In 2018, President Trump withdrew from the JCPOA, re-imposing U.S. sanctions.

Iran initially remained in the agreement, but resumed enrichment when European relief failed to materialize.

Military Escalation

As diplomacy collapsed, military tensions increased. Supreme Leader Ayatollah Ali Khamenei faced pressure to accelerate the program.

In June 2025, the U.S. air strikes on Iranian facilities aimed to delay nuclear progress, marking a serious military escalation.

The Ongoing Dilemma

The nuclear issue is unresolved. Iran insists on its right to peaceful nuclear technology, while Western powers view the program as a proliferation risk. Military strikes may delay but can't eliminate Iran's nuclear knowledge.

The question remains: Can diplomacy achieve a sustainable solution, or will the nuclear issue continue sparking confrontation, sanctions, and military action?

Common Misconceptions About Iran's International Relations

Misconception 1: Iran has always been hostile to the United States

Reality: Before 1979, Iran was a close U.S. ally. Hostility began with the revolution and the hostage crisis.

Misconception 2: Sanctions only hurt Iran's government

Reality: While targeting the regime, sanctions severely impact ordinary Iranians, affecting the economy and access to necessities.

Misconception 3: The 2015 nuclear deal allowed Iran to build nuclear weapons

Reality: The deal prohibited weapons development, imposing limits on enrichment and research.

Misconception 4: Iran's nuclear program began as a secret weapons project

Reality: The program started in the 1950s with U.S. support for peaceful purposes.

Misconception 5: The U.S. and Iran have never cooperated

Reality: Despite overall hostility, there have been instances of cooperation, such as against the Taliban and ISIS.

Quick Summary

Key Takeaways:

- The 1953 U.S.-backed coup against Mossadeq created lasting resentment.

- The 1979 revolution and hostage crisis severed diplomatic ties, establishing enduring hostility.

- Economic sanctions have severely damaged Iran's economy without fundamental policy changes.

- Iran's nuclear program, initially U.S.-supported, evolved into an international crisis.

- The 2015 nuclear deal was a diplomatic milestone but collapsed with U.S. withdrawal in 2018.

- Military confrontation has escalated significantly, with key figures targeted and facilities struck.

- The nuclear dilemma persists, with unresolved diplomatic and military challenges.

- Iran's isolation results from historical grievances and its own policies, shaping decision-making globally.

PART 7
WHY IRAN IS DIFFERENT

Chapter 21
Why Iran Never Lost Its Identity

Few civilizations have endured as many conquests and upheavals as Iran. From Arab armies in the seventh century to Mongol invasions and European interference, foreign powers repeatedly swept across Iranian lands. Yet through it all, Iran retained something remarkable: its cultural identity. While empires rose and fell, and religions changed, the Persian sense of self remained intact.

This chapter explores how Iran preserved its language, traditions, and distinct character across centuries of foreign rule. Understanding this resilience reveals not just Iranian history, but the power of culture to outlast political conquest. We will examine three key factors: the continuity of cultural practices, the preservation of language and tradition, and active resistance to assimilation.

Cultural Continuity

Iran's cultural identity survived because it was never fully erased by conquest. When Arab armies brought Islam to Persia in the seventh century, they changed the region's religion but not its soul. Unlike many conquered peoples who gradually adopted their conquerors' culture, Iranians maintained distinct practices, artistic traditions, and social structures.

The Sassanid era, which ended with the Arab conquest, had established strong cultural foundations. Persian art, architecture, literature, and administrative systems were sophisticated and deeply rooted. These elements didn't disappear overnight. Instead, they adapted and merged with new influences while maintaining their essential character.

Key Elements of Continuity:

- **Artistic traditions**: Persian miniature painting, carpet weaving, and architectural styles persisted through dynastic changes.

- **Administrative practices**: Persian bureaucratic systems influenced successive governments, including Arab caliphates.

- **Social customs**: Family structures, festivals, and daily life practices remained distinctly Persian.

- **Cultural memory**: Stories, legends, and historical narratives passed through generations.

The Safavid dynasty (1501–1736) marked a crucial turning point. Shah Ismail I unified Iran and established Shia Islam as the state religion, creating a distinct religious identity that separated Iran from its Sunni neighbors. This wasn't just a political move - it reinforced Iranian distinctiveness and provided a new framework for expressing Persian culture.

During the Safavid era, Iran experienced significant cultural, artistic, and political resurgence. Persian art flourished. Architecture reached new heights with stunning mosques and palaces in Isfahan. Literature thrived. This period demonstrated that Iranian culture could not only survive but actively flourish under the right conditions.

Even during the Qajar dynasty in the nineteenth century, when Russia and Great Britain exerted heavy influence and Iran lost territories, the core cultural identity remained. External pressure and territorial losses didn't translate into cultural erasure. Iranians continued to see themselves as heirs to an ancient, distinct civilization.

Language and Tradition

Language served as Iran's most powerful tool for cultural preservation. While Arabic became the language of religion and scholarship after the Arab conquest, Persian (Farsi) never died. Instead, it evolved and eventually reasserted itself as the primary language of literature, administration, and daily life.

By the ninth and tenth centuries, Persian literature experienced a remarkable revival. Poets wrote in Persian, not Arabic. The epic poem *Shahnameh* (Book of Kings) by Ferdowsi became a defining cultural monument, preserving pre-Islamic Iranian history and mythology in verse. This wasn't just literature - it was cultural resistance through storytelling.

Why Language Mattered:

- **Identity marker**: Speaking Persian distinguished Iranians from Arab conquerors and Turkish rulers.

- **Cultural transmission**: Language carried traditions, values, and historical memory across generations.

- **Literary tradition**: Persian poetry and prose created a shared cultural reference point.

- **Administrative continuity**: Persian remained the language of government in many periods.

Traditional practices also reinforced identity. Nowruz, the Persian New Year celebration with roots in Zoroastrian times, continued despite religious changes. This spring festival, with its specific rituals and symbolism, connected Iranians to their pre-Islamic past. It survived because it was deeply embedded in daily life and family traditions.

Other traditions persisted similarly. Persian music maintained distinct modes and instruments. Culinary traditions remained recognizably Persian. Social customs around hospitality, family relationships, and community life showed remarkable continuity.

The Safavid period strengthened these traditions by giving them official support. Persian became the language of the court. Traditional arts received royal patronage. Cultural practices were celebrated rather than suppressed. This institutional support helped ensure traditions would survive future challenges.

Even when foreign powers dominated politically, they often adopted Persian cultural elements rather than imposing their own. Mongol rulers, for example, eventually adopted Persian administrative practices and patronized Persian arts. This pattern repeated throughout Iranian history: conquerors became culturally "Persianized" rather than Persians becoming culturally absorbed.

Resistance to Assimilation

Iranian cultural survival wasn't passive - it involved active resistance to assimilation. This resistance took many forms, from subtle everyday choices to deliberate cultural movements.

After the Arab conquest, Iranians could have gradually adopted Arab identity, as happened in Egypt and North Africa. Instead, they maintained distinction. They learned Arabic for religious purposes but continued speaking Persian at home. They converted to Islam but interpreted it through Persian cultural lenses.

Forms of Resistance:

- **Literary movements**: Deliberate revival of Persian language in poetry and prose.

- **Religious differentiation**: Adoption of Shia Islam created religious distinction from Arab Sunni majority.

- **Historical consciousness**: Preservation of pre-Islamic history and heroes through storytelling.

- **Cultural pride**: Continued emphasis on Persian civilization's ancient achievements.

The establishment of Shia Islam as Iran's state religion under Shah Ismail I was partly a resistance strategy. By embracing a different branch of Islam than their neighbors, Iranians created a religious boundary that reinforced cultural boundaries. This wasn't just about theology - it was about maintaining distinctiveness.

During periods of foreign domination, cultural resistance became more subtle but no less important. Under Mongol rule, Persian bureaucrats and scholars maintained administrative systems and educational traditions. They preserved manuscripts, taught Persian literature, and kept cultural memory alive through difficult times.

The Qajar period presented different challenges. Russian and British influence threatened Iranian sovereignty. Territorial losses diminished Iran's physical boundaries. Yet cultural identity remained strong. Iranian intellectuals and reformers responded by emphasizing Persian heritage and calling for modernization that preserved Iranian character.

This resistance wasn't always organized or political. Often it was simply families teaching children Persian, communities celebrating traditional festivals, and individuals choosing to maintain customs. These small acts, multiplied across generations, proved more powerful than any conquest.

Common Misconceptions About Iranian Cultural Survival

Misconception 1: Arab conquest completely Arabized Iran

Reality: While Arabs brought Islam and Arabic became important for religious texts, Persian language and culture remained dominant in daily life and eventually reasserted themselves in literature and administration.

Misconception 2: Conversion to Islam erased pre-Islamic Iranian identity

Reality: Iranians maintained strong connections to pre-Islamic history through literature, festivals like Nowruz, and cultural memory. Islam was adapted to fit Persian cultural contexts.

Misconception 3: Iranian culture is simply "Islamic culture"

Reality: Iranian culture is distinct from Arab Islamic culture. Iran developed its own artistic styles, literary traditions, and religious interpretation (Shia Islam) that reflect Persian heritage.

Misconception 4: Foreign rulers successfully imposed their cultures on Iran

Reality: Throughout history, foreign rulers often became "Persianized," adopting Persian administrative practices, patronizing Persian arts, and using the Persian language, rather than successfully imposing their own cultures.

Misconception 5: Cultural survival was automatic or inevitable

Reality: Iranian cultural continuity required active effort - deliberate preservation of language, conscious maintenance of traditions, and resistance to assimilation across many generations.

Quick Summary

Key Takeaways:

- Iran maintained cultural identity through multiple conquests by Arabs, Mongols, Turks, and European powers from the 7th century onward.

- Persian language survived and eventually flourished despite Arabic's religious dominance, serving as the primary vehicle for cultural preservation.

- The Safavid dynasty (1501–1736) strengthened Iranian identity by establishing Shia Islam as the state religion, creating religious distinction from neighbors.

- Traditional practices like Nowruz and Persian artistic traditions provided continuity linking modern Iran to ancient Persia.

- Cultural resistance took many forms: literary revivals, maintenance of Persian in administration, preservation of pre-Islamic history, and everyday choices by families and communities.

- Foreign conquerors often became "Persianized" rather than successfully assimilating Iranians into their cultures.

- Shah Ismail I played a crucial role in unifying Iran and establishing a distinctive religious identity in the early 16th century.

- Even during periods of foreign domination and territorial loss (like the Qajar dynasty in the 19th century), core cultural identity remained intact.

Chapter 22
Religion, Power, and the West

The Iranian Revolution of 1978–1979 transformed Iran and reshaped the interplay between religion and politics in the Middle East. The fall of the monarchy on February 11, 1979, heralded the rise of the world's first modern Islamic republic, where religious authority gained supreme political power.

This chapter explores how Shi'a Islam became the cornerstone of revolutionary identity, how religious leaders wielded unprecedented political authority, and how Iran's new regime opposed Western influence.

Understanding these dynamics is crucial to grasping the ongoing political tensions in the Middle East. We'll examine the role of Shi'a Islam in unifying diverse groups, the mechanisms through which religious figures exercised power, and the ideological conflicts that emerged between Iran and the West.

The Role of Shi'a Islam

Shi'a Islam provided the cultural and ideological backbone of the Iranian Revolution. Unlike movements driven by nationalism or class struggle, this revolution united a diverse array of social groups—students, merchants, workers, intellectuals, and clerics - under a shared religious identity.

Religious Unity Across Social Classes

The revolution succeeded because Shi'i Islam offered a common language and symbols that transcended economic and social divides. Religious slogans, particularly *Allāhu akbar* (God is greatest), resonated from rooftops across Iranian cities, serving as political statements of defiance against the shah's regime.

Khomeini's Mobilization Strategy

Ruhollah Khomeini, a religious scholar critical of the shah for years, emerged as the revolution's spiritual and political leader. His speeches outlined a vision of governance by religious authority instead of secular monarchy. Khomeini's message linked religious devotion with political liberation.

Shi'a Identity as Revolutionary Fuel

The historical narrative of resistance and martyrdom in Shi'a Islam, especially Imam Husayn's stand against tyranny, provided powerful symbolism for the revolutionaries. Political opposition was reframed as a matter of faith, turning participation into a religious duty.

Post-Revolutionary Influence

After the monarchy's fall, Shi'i Islam became the state's organizing principle. The concept of *velayet-i faqih* (guardianship of the jurist) positioned religious scholars as ultimate political authorities, fundamentally reshaping Iran's governance.

Religion as Political Power

The Iranian Revolution introduced a government model where religious authority held direct political control, merging mosque and state uniquely in the modern world.

The Doctrine of Velayet-i Faqih

Khomeini's political philosophy, *velayet-i faqih*, argued for Islamic jurists to govern society in the absence of the Hidden Imam. This doctrine granted religious scholars constitutional power in state matters.

Constitutional Structure

The new constitution established a dual system with elected bodies like a president and parliament, but ultimate authority rested with the

Supreme Leader - a senior religious scholar. This ensured that religious interpretation guided major policies.

Evolution of Revolutionary Ideals

The political system that emerged was not a direct implementation of Khomeini's original vision. The constitution involved compromises and adaptations, creating a complex government where religious and republican elements coexisted.

Domestic Policy Impact

Post-revolution, religious authority influenced all aspects of life. Laws aligned with Islamic principles, impacting social policies, education, and cultural expression. The state enforced religious codes of conduct on dress and public behavior.

The Shiite Crescent Concept

Iran's influence extended beyond its borders through the idea of a "Shiite crescent" - a network of Shi'a communities across the Middle East. Iran positioned itself as the protector of Shi'a populations, using religious solidarity for regional influence.

Tensions with Western Nations

The Islamic Republic's founding principles put it in ideological conflict with Western powers, particularly the United States, shaping Iran's foreign policy.

Anti-Western Ideology

The revolution, in part, responded to the shah's close ties with the West, especially the U.S. Revolutionaries saw the shah as a puppet of foreign powers imposing Western models on Iran. The new government opposed this, positioning itself as anti-imperialist.

Opposition to Western Policies

Post-revolution Iran actively opposed Western influence in the Muslim world. The government framed its foreign policy as supporting oppressed people against Western imperialism, supporting various resistance movements.

The White Revolution's Legacy

Much anti-Western sentiment stemmed from the shah's "White Revolution" - modernization reforms in the 1960s and 1970s backed by Western powers. These reforms disrupted traditional structures and created economic inequalities, fueling resentment.

Regional Influence Strategy

Iran aimed to export its revolutionary ideology, supporting groups it saw as oppressed, especially Shi'a communities. This led to conflicts with Western-aligned governments and powers in the region.

Lasting Diplomatic Isolation

The ideological divide led to lasting diplomatic tensions, sanctions, and periodic military conflicts. Iran's rejection of Western norms and its support for anti-Western movements have resulted in sustained mutual suspicion.

Common Misconceptions

Misconception 1: The Iranian Revolution was purely religious

While Shi'a Islam unified the movement, it had diverse causes like economic grievances and opposition to authoritarianism. Different groups participated for varied reasons.

Misconception 2: Khomeini's vision was immediately implemented

The post-revolution government evolved through negotiations and compromises. The final system differed from Khomeini's original ideas, blending religious and republican elements.

Misconception 3: All Iranians supported the Islamic Republic

Though diverse groups united against the shah, consensus faded after the monarchy fell, with many secular participants opposing the new government's direction.

Misconception 4: Iran's conflict with the West is ancient

Modern tensions arose mainly from 20th-century events - particularly the shah's Western alignment and the revolution's rejection of it—rather than ancient religious wars.

Misconception 5: Shi'a Islam automatically means political Islam

Iran's model of religious governance is specific to its revolutionary context. Most Shi'a Muslims worldwide do not experience similar systems, and many scholars have historically opposed clerical rule.

Quick Summary

Key Takeaways:

- **Shi'a Islam unified diverse groups** during the 1978–1979 Iranian Revolution through shared religious identity.

- **Ruhollah Khomeini envisioned government** led by religious scholars, merging spiritual and political authority.

- **The revolution toppled the monarchy** on February 11, 1979, establishing the Islamic Republic of Iran.

- **Velayet-i faqih gave religious jurists** constitutional power, creating a system where clerics held ultimate authority.

- **The new government opposed Western influence**, seeing the shah's ties with Western powers as a primary grievance.

- **Iran's foreign policy was shaped** by Shiite identity, supporting groups seen as oppressed in the Muslim world.

- **Anti-Western sentiment stemmed** from opposition to the White Revolution's reforms and perceived foreign interference.

- **The Shiite crescent concept** extended Iran's influence across regional Shi'a communities, fostering a network of religious and political solidarity.

Chapter 23
The 2,500 Year Pattern

Iran's history reveals a remarkable truth: few civilizations have endured so many catastrophic invasions while maintaining a distinct cultural identity. Over 2,500 years, Iran has been conquered by Greeks, Arabs, Turks, and Mongols. Empires have risen and fallen on its soil, yet through each upheaval, a continuous thread of Iranian identity, language, and culture has persisted.

This chapter examines the recurring patterns in Iranian history: cycles of political rise and collapse, waves of foreign invasion followed by cultural absorption, and the enduring persistence of Iranian civilization. Understanding these patterns explains not only Iran's past but also its present resilience and sense of historical continuity.

What makes Iran different from other conquered lands? Why did Iranian culture survive when so many others disappeared? The answers lie in geography, cultural strength, and a unique ability to transform conquerors into Iranians.

Cycles of Rise and Fall

Iranian history follows a recognizable pattern: powerful dynasties emerge, expand their territories, reach a peak, and then gradually weaken and collapse. This cycle has repeated for over two millennia.

The Pattern of Imperial Rise

Each major Iranian dynasty began with military strength and political consolidation. The Achaemenids (550–330 BCE) built the first Persian Empire through conquest and administrative genius. Centuries later, the Sassanians (224–651 CE) restored Iranian power with a sophisticated imperial system. After the Arab conquest, the Safavids (1501–1736) reunified Iran, establishing Shia Islam as the state religion.

These dynasties shared key features: strong founding rulers, effective bureaucracies, and cultural flourishing. They built magnificent cities, sponsored arts and literature, and expanded trade networks.

The Collapse Pattern

Yet each dynasty eventually weakened due to:

- Succession disputes and civil wars

- Economic strain from military campaigns

- Administrative corruption and inefficiency

- External military pressure

- Regional fragmentation and rebellion

The Achaemenid Empire succumbed to Alexander the Great in 334 BCE, the Sassanians fell under Arab invasion in the 7th century, and the Safavids lost control over provinces in the 18th century.

Modern Cycles

This pattern continued into modern times. The Pahlavi dynasty (1925–1979) rose through military strength, pursued rapid modernization, then collapsed amid revolution. The cycle of rise, peak achievement, and fall remained constant across vastly different historical periods.

Understanding this pattern helps explain Iranian political culture: awareness of past glory, expectation of eventual decline, and determination to rebuild after collapse.

Foreign Invasions and Recovery

Iran's strategic geography - situated between Central Asia, the Middle East, and South Asia - made it a perpetual target for conquest. Yet remarkably, Iran absorbed its conquerors rather than disappearing under their rule.

Major Invasions

Iran faced four particularly devastating invasions:

- **Alexander the Great (334 BCE)**: The Macedonian conqueror destroyed the Achaemenid Empire, burning Persepolis and ending Persian political independence for centuries.

- **Arab Conquest (7th century CE)**: Muslim armies defeated the Sassanians, introducing Islam and Arabic script while ending Zoroastrian dominance.

- **Mongol Invasions (13th century)**: Genghis Khan and his successors devastated Iranian cities, causing population loss and economic destruction.

- **Tamerlane's Campaigns (1220 CE and later)**: This Central Asian conqueror repeatedly invaded Iran, destroying cities and massacring populations.

Each invasion brought catastrophic consequences: destroyed cities, massacred populations, collapsed economies, and political fragmentation.

The Pattern of Cultural Recovery

Yet Iran displayed a remarkable pattern of cultural resilience. Within generations of each conquest, Iranian culture began reasserting itself:

The Greeks who ruled after Alexander adopted Persian administrative practices. Arab conquerors brought Islam, but Iranians shaped it into distinct Persian Islamic traditions. Mongol rulers became patrons of Persian culture within decades, adopting Persian as the administrative language. Tamerlane, despite his brutality, sponsored Persian arts and literature.

Why Iran Survived

Several factors explain this resilience:

- Strong pre-existing cultural identity and literary tradition

- Sophisticated administrative systems that conquerors needed

- Persian language's prestige and utility

- Geographic continuity and distinct boundaries

- Cultural flexibility that absorbed foreign elements while maintaining core identity

Iran didn't just survive invasions - it culturally absorbed its conquerors, turning military defeats into long-term cultural victories.

The Persistence of Iran

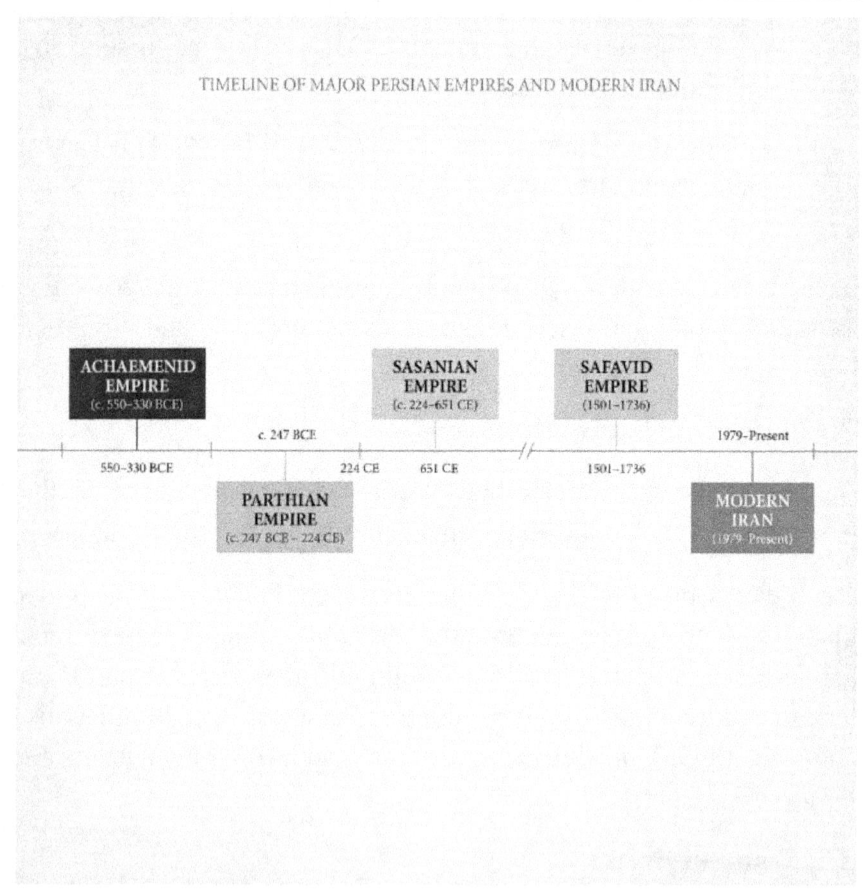

Timeline graphic of Persian empires

The most striking feature of Iranian history is continuity. Despite political fragmentation, foreign rule, and repeated catastrophes, Iran maintained a distinct identity across 2,500 years.

Elements of Continuity

Several factors contributed to this persistence:

Language: Persian (Farsi) survived as a living language despite foreign rule. Even when Arabic became the religious language, Persian remained the language of literature, administration, and daily life. This linguistic continuity preserved cultural memory and identity.

Cultural Memory: Iranians maintained awareness of their pre-Islamic past. The *Shahnameh* (Book of Kings), completed around 1010 CE, preserved ancient Iranian legends, keeping pre-Islamic identity alive under Islamic rule.

Geographic Identity: Iran's natural boundaries - mountains, deserts, and seas - created a distinct geographic space, maintaining a sense of territorial continuity even when political control fragmented.

Administrative Traditions: Persian bureaucratic systems were so effective that conquerors adopted them, maintaining institutional memory and practices across dynasties.

Cultural Prestige: Persian culture - its poetry, art, architecture, and courtly traditions - commanded respect; foreign rulers adopted rather than replaced it.

Modern Persistence

This pattern continued into the modern era. The Pahlavi dynasty attempted rapid Westernization, yet traditional Iranian identity persisted. The 1979 Revolution, despite its break with the monarchy, drew heavily on historical consciousness and national identity.

Today, Iranians reference ancient empires, classical poetry, and historical continuity as sources of national pride. The 2,500-year pattern remains relevant to contemporary Iranian self-understanding.

The Iranian Exception

Few civilizations have maintained such continuity. Egypt lost its ancient language and identity. Mesopotamia disappeared as a distinct culture. Yet Iran survived as Iran - transformed by history but recognizably continuous with its ancient past.

This persistence resulted from conscious cultural preservation, geographic advantages, and a sophisticated civilization more durable than the empires that tried to conquer it.

Common Misconceptions About Iranian Historical Patterns

Misconception 1: Iran Has Always Been Politically Unified

Reality: Iran experienced long periods of fragmentation. Political unity was the exception, not the rule. Cultural unity persisted even when political control fragmented.

Misconception 2: Foreign Invasions Destroyed Iranian Culture

Reality: While invasions caused immediate devastation, Iranian culture reasserted itself. Conquerors typically adopted Persian culture rather than replacing it. Cultural defeats often became long-term cultural victories.

Misconception 3: The Arab Conquest Ended Iranian Identity

Reality: The Arab conquest introduced Islam but didn't erase Iranian identity. Iranians developed a distinct Persian Islamic culture and eventually established Shia Islam as a marker of Iranian distinctiveness.

Misconception 4: Iranian History Is Simply a Series of Empires

Reality: The pattern is more complex - cycles of imperial consolidation, cultural flowering, political collapse, foreign invasion, and cultural recovery. Understanding the full cycle is essential to grasping Iranian history.

Misconception 5: Modern Iran Has No Connection to Ancient Persia

Reality: Modern Iranians maintain strong consciousness of their pre-Islamic past. Ancient sites, classical literature, and historical memory remain important to contemporary identity, creating genuine continuity across millennia.

Quick Summary

Key Takeaways:

- Iranian history follows a recurring pattern: dynastic rise, cultural achievement, political collapse, and recovery.

- Major invasions by Alexander the Great, Arabs, Mongols, and Tamerlane devastated Iran but didn't destroy its cultural identity.

- Iran consistently absorbed its conquerors, who adopted Persian language, administrative systems, and cultural practices.

- Linguistic continuity, cultural prestige, geographic boundaries, and historical memory enabled Iran to maintain its identity across 2,500 years.

- The Pahlavi dynasty represented a modern iteration of traditional patterns: rapid rise, transformation attempts, and eventual collapse.

- Iran's strategic geography made it a constant target for invasion while its cultural sophistication made it resilient against cultural erasure.

- Few civilizations have maintained such continuity - Iran survived as a distinct culture when many others disappeared.

- Understanding these patterns explains both Iran's historical resilience and its contemporary sense of identity rooted in ancient continuity.

Chapter 24
The Future of Iran

Iran stands at a crossroads. After more than four decades under the Islamic Republic, the nation faces profound challenges that will shape its trajectory for generations. Economic pressures, social tensions, and geopolitical conflicts have created an environment filled with both uncertainty and possibility. To comprehend Iran's current situation, one must examine the political shifts, economic struggles, and social movements that have defined recent decades.

This chapter explores where Iran stands today, considers possible paths forward, and reflects on what the nation's complex history reveals about its future. The patterns of the past forty years - cycles of reform and retrenchment, engagement and isolation - offer important clues about what may come next.

Iran Today

The Political Landscape

Since the Islamic Revolution of 1979, Iran's political system has vacillated between periods of relative openness and conservative entrenchment. This pattern has shaped the nation's modern trajectory.

The reformist movement gained momentum in the late 1990s when Mohammad Khatami won the presidency in 1997, initiating a period of cautious liberalization. Reformists achieved significant electoral victories, reflecting widespread public desire for greater freedoms and economic opportunities.

However, the Guardian Council - a powerful body that vets candidates and legislation - consistently limited reformist ambitions, and by 2004, conservatives had regained control, demonstrating the system's built-in mechanisms for maintaining ideological boundaries.

Mahmoud Ahmedinejad's presidency marked a return to hardline policies, characterized by increased international isolation and domestic repression. The 2009 presidential election prompted the Green Uprising after widespread claims of electoral fraud, revealing deep fractures in Iranian society.

Hassan Rouhani's presidency brought renewed hopes for reform, particularly through the 2015 nuclear agreement. However, the U.S. withdrawal from the agreement under President Donald Trump devastated these prospects. The assassination of General Qassem Soleimani by the U.S. in 2020 further escalated tensions. When Ibrahim Raisi, an ultraconservative, won the presidency in 2021, it marked a shift toward conservative control.

Economic Challenges

Economic instability remains Iran's most pressing domestic issue. High inflation has eroded living standards, while international sanctions targeting oil exports and banking systems have severely constrained economic growth. The collapse of the nuclear agreement dashed hopes for sanctions relief, leading to significant currency devaluation and persistent unemployment, particularly among young people.

These economic pressures fuel social discontent, with many Iranians seeing limited opportunities for advancement. The situation has led to a brain drain as educated professionals seek opportunities abroad.

Social Movements and Protests

In 2022, Iran experienced its largest protests since 1979, sparked by the death of Mahsa Amini in police custody. The protests reflected deep frustration with social restrictions, economic hardship, and political repression. Women played particularly prominent roles, and the slogan "Woman, Life, Freedom" became a rallying cry. These demonstrations revealed the widening gap between the government and significant portions of the population, especially younger Iranians.

Regional Conflicts

Iran's regional position is increasingly complex. The 2023 Hamas attack on Israel sparked a broader conflict involving Iranian-backed groups. These developments have heightened tensions with Israel and the U.S. while strengthening Iran's ties with Russia and China. Iran's support for proxy forces has extended its influence but also made it a target for regional rivals, with significant economic and diplomatic costs.

Possible Futures

Scenario One: Gradual Reform

One possible future involves gradual political and social liberalization, with reformist and centrist figures gaining influence and pushing for incremental changes. This path might include relaxation of social restrictions, limited economic reforms, and cautious engagement with Western nations.

Despite its appeal, this scenario faces significant obstacles. The Guardian Council and Supreme Leader Ayatollah Ali Khamenei have consistently blocked major reforms. Reformists struggle to mobilize voters who have grown cynical about change.

Scenario Two: Continued Hardline Control

Another possibility involves sustained conservative control, characterized by increased social restrictions, confrontation with Western powers, and deeper ties with non-Western nations. While maintaining stability in the short term, this path could increase long-term risks, including more explosive social unrest and deeper international isolation.

The succession of Supreme Leader Khamenei is a critical factor. Power struggles among conservative factions could destabilize the system.

Scenario Three: Revolutionary Change

A more dramatic possibility involves fundamental transformation. The 2022 protests indicate that many, especially younger Iranians, desire systemic change. Revolutionary change could come through sustained protests, economic collapse, military intervention, or regional conflicts.

This scenario carries enormous risks. The security apparatus is powerful and likely to resist change violently.

Scenario Four: Negotiated Transition

A fourth possibility involves a negotiated political transition, with reformists, conservatives, and civil society groups reaching accommodation on democratization. Constitutional reforms and engagement with Western nations might be possible under such a scenario.

However, the deep mistrust between government and opposition, along with international tensions, makes this scenario difficult to envision in the near term.

Final Reflections

Modern skyline of Tehran

Lessons from History

Iran's history offers lessons for understanding its future. The nation has experienced dramatic transformations influenced by both internal dynamics and external pressures. Foreign intervention has repeatedly shaped Iranian politics, and this pattern continues today.

Despite political upheavals, cultural continuity has persisted. Persian language, literary traditions, and national identity have survived conquest, revolution, and repression.

The Weight of Expectations

The Islamic Republic faces a gap between revolutionary promises and reality, with many questioning whether promises of justice and governance have been fulfilled. Younger Iranians judge the regime against their aspirations and opportunities seen in other nations, fundamentally altering the political equation.

The Regional Context

Iran's future is intertwined with Middle Eastern dynamics. The collapse of traditional power structures creates both dangers and opportunities. Iran's complex relations with neighbors remain a pivotal factor.

The Question of Identity

Iran's future hinges on unresolved questions of national identity. The balance between Islamic governance and Persian nationalism remains contentious, with different societal segments holding competing visions.

Reasons for Hope

Despite challenges, reasons for hope exist. Iran's human capital and cultural heritage provide foundations for potential unity and resilience. The younger generation's demands for change reflect healthy civic engagement.

The Path Forward

Iran's future is unwritten. The nation faces genuine choices regarding its political, economic, and social paths. These choices will be made by Iranians themselves, influenced but not determined by external actors. History suggests Iran will continue to defy expectations, combining continuity and change in unique ways.

Key Takeaways

- Iran's political system has oscillated between reformist and conservative control, with conservatives currently dominant.

- Economic challenges, particularly high inflation and international sanctions, create significant pressure for change.

- The 2022 protests revealed deep social tensions.

- Multiple possible futures exist, each with distinct challenges and risks.

- Generational change is reshaping Iranian politics.

- Iran's regional conflicts complicate domestic challenges.

- The succession of Supreme Leader Khamenei will critically shape Iran's trajectory.

- Iranian society's resilience and cultural strength provide foundations for navigating future challenges.

Congratulations! you've just completed a journey through more than 2,500 years of history.

That's no small achievement.

By reaching the end, you've gained a deeper understanding of Iran - its empires, its transformations, and the forces that continue to shape it today. Few readers make it this far, and your curiosity and commitment truly set you apart.

If you found this book helpful or engaging, I'd really appreciate it if you could take a moment to leave a review. Even a short review makes a big difference - it helps other readers discover the book and supports the creation of future titles.

Thank you for reading - and well done for finishing ☺